TREASURES

IN CROSS-STITCH

TREASURES
IN CROSS-STITCH

Jane Greenoff

THE QUILT DIGEST PRESS
Simply the Best from NTC Publishing Group
Lincolnwood, Illinois U.S.A.

Illustrations by Ethan Danielson
Photographs by Di Lewis
Manufactured in Great Britain

Library of Congress Cataloging-in-Publication Data

Greenoff, Jane
Treasures in Cross-stitch / Jane Greenoff
p. cm.
Includes bibliographical references and index.
1. Cross-stitch 2. Cross-stitch-Patterns.   I Title.
TT778.C76G7523 1996
746.44'3041-dc20   95-52797
CIP

Published by The Quilt Digest Press,
a division of NTC Publishing Group,
4255 West Touhy Avenue,
Lincolnwood (Chicago), Illinois 60646-1975, U.S.A.

By arrangement with BBC Books, BBC Worldwide Ltd,
Woodlands, 80 Wood Lane, London W12 0TT.
Original English Language Version

To my husband Bill,
who knows why I always dedicate my books to him

Contents

Acknowledgements

I would like to thank all the people and organizations without whose support this book would never have been written. A very special thank you to my all-suffering husband, Bill, who has checked patterns, read proofs and just been there when I needed him, and to my children, James and Louise, who didn't complain about having junk food again and again.

I would also like to thank: Michel Standley and all at our company, The Inglestone Collection, who kept the business thriving all year round; my special friend and business associate, Sue Hawkins, whose finishing service is second to none – this book would have been the poorer without her friendship and expertise – (Contact Needleworks, The Old School House, Hall Road, Leckhampton, Cheltenham, Glos); Ian Lawson-Smith and all at I. L. Soft Witney, England, for my wonderful cross-stitch design programme which made this book possible and for all their support, often above and beyond the call of duty! Terry Belanger for teaching me so much during my visit to South Carolina and Ethan Danielson for making sense of the cross-stitch charts.

A special thank you to my marvellous team of stitchers who stitch under pressure and enjoy it, check patterns, make sense of my scribbles and contribute their ideas and suggestions, both for book projects and often our kit company. They are: Dorothy Presley, Barbara Webster, Hanne Castelo, Jenny Kirby, Hanne Lise Stamper, Sarah Day, Margaret Cornish, Jill Vaughan, Sophie Bartlett, Carol Lebez, Kathy Elliot, Sharon Griffiths, Vera Greenoff, Sarah Haines, Su Maddocks, Trina Tait, Glenys Thorne, Lynn Robinson, Angie Davidson, Suzanne Hunt, Lesley Clegg and Christine Banfield.

For supplies of threads, fabrics and equipment: Gary Borrow, Simply Scissors, Midholm, London, for the pretty stork scissors; Cara Ackerman at DMC Creative World for fabric and threads; Len and Malcolm Turner of Fabric Flair Ltd for plentiful supplies of Jobelan; Clive and Rosemary Sheridan, Wye Needlecraft, Bakewell, Derbyshire; Peter and Rosemary Lundgren, Hemsleys, Lincoln, for their enthusiasm and support; Liberty of London for patterned and decorative fabrics and particularly Mrs Amanda Hutchinson for her continued help and advice.

For frames and cards: Tunley and Son Ltd, Swindon, for lovely frames; Leverton Frames, Hungerford, for the super cherub frame; Sudberry House, Old Lyme, CT 06371, USA, for Shaker box and small wooden clock cupboard.

For beads and charms: Framecraft Miniatures, Birmingham, England, for supplies of Mill Hill beads; Beadcraft, High Wycombe, England, for sequins; The Rocking Rabbit Trading Company, Newmarket, Suffolk, for gold- and silver-coloured charms.

For beautiful furniture: Magregor Designs, Burton on Trent, for kindly supplying the lovely dark wood firescreen and the small wooden pincushion, and Roland Bartlett, Jar Frames for the needlework box and large footstool.

Joyce Nightingale who thought of me when selling her crewel panel; Ken and Ginnie Thompson who taught me so much; Jo Verso who introduced me to crazy patchwork; Dougal Benzie for help with the charts; our American distributors Margy Richardson and Susan Burge of Designing Women Unlimited, who have given me such support over the last year; and Carma and all her team at The Counting House, South Carolina, just for being there!

A special thank you to Meg Shinall for the gift of her beautiful book *Seventeenth-century Band Sampler* (see Further Reading, page 157), to Pat Carson of Gloria & Pat for all her support, and to all the museums, galleries and individuals who contributed their time and expertise in the preparation of this book.

JANE GREENOFF
AND THE INGLESTONE COLLECTION

Jane discovered counted cross-stitch through a neighbour and within six months had marketed her first design, having perceived a gap in the market for a genuinely English product. Thus the Inglestone Collection began and was the first company in the UK to gold-plate tapestry and cross-stitch needles, and has the only British working paper-perforator which was made for the manufacture of stitching paper.

The Inglestone Collection produces Jane Greenoff's counted cross-stitch kits and charts, including some of the designs in this and her other books. These designs are available from most good needlework shops or, in case of difficulty, by mail order. Black-and-white charts are available for the designs in this book should you require them. Please telephone for details. Ask at your local needlework shop for details or write (enclosing a stamped addressed envelope) to Jane Greenoff's Inglestone Collection, Yells Yard, Cirencester Road, Fairford, Glos GL7 4BS or telephone 01285 712778.

In the USA, Jane Greenoff's books and kits are available from Designing Women Unlimited, 601 East 8th Street, El Dorado, Arkansas 71730, USA (telephone: 501 862 0021).

THE CROSS STITCH GUILD

THE CROSS STITCH GUILD

Jane Greenoff founded the Guild in 1996 to promote the enjoyment of counted needlework of all kinds. Guild membership has the benefit of regular journals, study folios, access to the Guild Members Room at Longleat and and discounts from the Guild Retails Partners. Members can contribute to influence various parts of the needlework industry - design, manufacture, retailing and publishing, etc. but also share the fun of it all with other stitchers, hence the Guild motto 'Together, We Count'. For details of subscriptions, member facilities and any other details, contact: The Cross Stitch Guild, The Stable Courtyard, Longleat House, Warminster BA12 7NL Telephone: 01985 844774.

Introduction

This book grew from my love of needlework and travel. Any journey, whether a family holiday or a business trip, has given me the excuse to visit museums, stately homes, and private collections of embroidery and furnishings. I never fail to find at least one *treasure* which gives me that special tingle! It may be the fineness of the workmanship, the coloured silks and golden threads, the techniques used or just the pure beauty of the finished piece that can take my breath away.

I never cease to be surprised when visiting a tiny church or village hall, to see embroidered banners or canvas work kneelers of such beauty, lying unannounced in a corner. If these works of art – and that is certainly what they are – were paintings, they would be in a vault somewhere. I look at the stitches and marvel at the accuracy and perfection achieved without the use of electric light and illuminated magnifier!

Since I have made needlework an all-consuming passion and cross-stitch my living, I have travelled around Europe and the United States of America, on my own as well as with my family, and continue to enjoy the friendship and mutual pleasure of needlework enthusiasts. During the last five years I have both attended and given classes all over the United Kingdom and America and continue to learn more about this gentle craft. I have listened to the expert and novice alike and the final section of this book bears testament to this. Both the basic cross-stitch instructions and the specific stitch instructions are personal and have been developed over hundreds of hours of designing and stitching. I hope they are simple to read, clear and jargon-free and that they increase your enjoyment from this, my twelfth, book!

The designs in the following pages were inspired by one or more pieces of antique needlework either from my own collection, or from museums or private collections in Europe and the USA. Each chapter or section is loosely based on a real historical source, which is adapted to suit the cross-stitch medium and charted in full colour for each project. As you will see from the beautiful colour photographs throughout the book, these designs may be stitched as single large projects or used as motifs for smaller pieces and made up as wonderful gifts or pictures and objects for your home.

I am not an embroiderer and cannot claim to be able to copy exactly these works of art, but I am a passionate stitcher who loves to learn. This book is aimed at lovers of needlework and the cross-stitcher in particular. The designs charted for you to reproduce are not copies of old needlework but are inspired by, and in the style of, the original pieces. All the projects may be reproduced in cross-stitch although in some cases I have added traditional counted stitches, including Algerian eye, French knots, hollie point, bullion knots, long-legged cross-stitch, double cross-stitch, satin stitch, herringbone stitch, queen stitch and back-stitch.

Cross-stitch is enjoying greater popularity now than many years ago and although the fabrics, threads and equipment used by the stitcher are modern, cross-stitch has been recorded for centuries. Examples of cross-stitch counted onto fabric were discovered among the treasures uncovered in the Pyramids and the stitch has been included as part of costume and decoration all over the world. The most exciting fact about cross-stitch is that anyone can do it – it is so simple! The only limit to the stitch is your eyesight and your imagination. As I stitch under my daylight bulb in the comfort of my centrally-heated home, I try to imagine Anne Boleyn or Catherine Parr stitching by candlelight at Sudeley Castle hundreds of years ago and can only wonder at their skill.

Counted needlework and particularly cross-stitch is a sympathetic craft and allows both the novice and the expert to tackle the same project, but enables the more experienced, confident stitcher to develop his or her technique using traditional fabrics and composite stitches (see Additional stitches, page 23).

To help you tackle the designs in this book I have graded the projects into skill levels 1–5 and given fabric suggestions. For example, a project graded skill level 1 using Aida fabric would be perfect for your first counted cross-stitch project. Skill level 5 using fine linen and including composite stitches is intended for the more experienced stitcher. In all cases it is possible to simplify a design and work it in pure cross-stitch and thus adapt it to suit your skill level.

If you are new to counted needlework, allow me to make one suggestion. For your first attempt at counted cross-stitch, select a fabric that you can see clearly and count easily, perfect your first stitches and complete that first project. You will be your own harshest critic and you can move to finer fabrics as you learn. You may prefer the effect of fine linen and even silk gauze, but it is so disheartening to learn the techniques while struggling to see the material!

The hardest parts of writing this book were choosing which pieces of antique embroidery to exclude and how best to share all the glorious examples of embroidery that I have been privileged to find. As always the choices were extremely difficult to make, so I have attempted to illustrate my love of this gentle rewarding craft with a wide variety of designs, styles and subject matter and hope that you will enjoy stitching from these pages as much as I have relished designing and stitching them.

How to use this book

....

The main content of the book is divided into nineteen sections, each one including one or more new projects based on an original antique piece. Each section includes a colour chart, lists of requirements and detailed instructions to make the worked examples as shown in the colour photographs. Basic cross-stitch instructions and special stitches are included in the first section of this book and the finishing techniques at the back of the book.

The design size included in each section refers to the example in the colour photograph so it is vital that if you alter the fabric type, thread count or design, you check the new design size before cutting the fabric. Refer to Calculating design size on page 21 if you are unsure. Many of the projects are interchangeable but there are a few which are not suitable for Aida-style fabric. In the stitching notes at the beginning of each project, I have indicated whether an even-weave material is essential or could be substituted with Aida. (When referring to even-weave fabric, linen, Jobelan or Linda may be used.)

The charts are made up of coloured squares some with an additional symbol to aid colour identification. You will see from the charts that I have added a solid line around many of the motifs which may be used as optional back-stitch outline, but it is also invaluable when planning your own designs and mixing motifs from different sections. In most cases the design may be worked straight from the illustrated chart although with some of the large designs, you will need to make a simple layout chart to position the individual motifs before starting to stitch (see Planning layout charts, page 21).

All the designs illustrated in the glorious colour photographs were stitched using DMC stranded cotton (floss) so that if you wish to reproduce my worked examples, you will need to select the DMC shade included on the coloured chart. I have included the Anchor/Bates alternative shade numbers, although an exact match is not always possible.

All the dimensions are given in metric with the imperial measurements in brackets. These are approximate conversions so please avoid mixing the two.

I have relished learning new techniques and designing and stitching the projects for this very personal book. May you have as much pleasure from it as I have. Happy stitching!

Basic Techniques

Cross-stitch Explained

The designs in this book are worked from charts in counted cross-stitch, although I have introduced a few different stitches and techniques to echo some of the historical source material that has inspired the designs. All the designs may be adapted to suit basic cross-stitch, although some of the projects are not intended for Aida material but require an even-weave material to achieve the most satisfying results. The following section deals with the materials and equipment needed and the techniques necessary for counted needlework.

Fabrics

All counted designs are made up of squares or parts of squares. The principle is that the picture, pattern or motif is transferred onto the fabric by matching the weave of the fabric to the pattern or chart. The term 'counted' means that the design is transferred onto the fabric by counting the squares on the chart and matching these on the fabric so that each stitch will be put in the right place.

The fabrics used for counted cross-stitch are all woven so that they have the same number of threads or blocks to 2.5 cm (1 inch) in both directions. The warp (vertical threads) and weft (horizontal threads) are woven evenly so that when a stitch is formed it will appear as a square or part of a square.

When choosing fabrics for counted cross-stitch, the thread count is the method used by manufacturers to differentiate between the varieties available; the higher the number or the more threads or stitches to 2.5 cm (1 inch), the finer the fabric.

Aida

This excellent cotton fabric is woven for counted needlework and is ideal for the beginner. The threads are woven in blocks rather than singly. There are many projects that suit this fabric particularly well as it forms a very pretty square stitch. Aida is available in 8, 11, 14, 16 and 18 blocks to 2.5 cm (1 inch) and if you require an even finer stitch count, it is possible to use Hardanger fabric at 22 blocks to 2.5 cm (1 inch).

When stitching on Aida, one block on the fabric corresponds to one square on the chart. Working a cross-stitch on Aida is exactly the same as on linen except that instead of counting threads, you count the single blocks. Forming three-quarter stitches on Aida is less accurate than on linen, but if you select one of the softer, less dressed varieties it can work well (see the Stars panel on page 31).

Aida is available in a wide variety of solid colours and now in rustic mixtures which add an antique feel to this modern fabric (see design on pages 118 and 134).

Cross-stitch on Aida

17

Linen

This lovely, if slightly more expensive, material made from flax is commonly used for counted cross-stitch. Stitching on linen is no more complicated than stitching on Aida – it just requires a different technique. Linen has irregularities in the fabric, which occur naturally and add to the charm of the finished piece, and is ideal when you are trying to emulate the style of an antique piece.

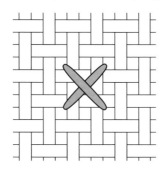

Cross-stitch on linen

To even out any discrepancies, cross-stitches are generally worked over two threads of the fabric in each direction, although I have broken this rule in this book! You will see in The Lovers Sampler (page 68) I have added extra detail to the people's faces by working over one thread, thus doubling the number of stitches available.

Linen is generally available in white, antique white, cream, raw or natural shades and now in a variety of colours.

Jobelan

Jobelan is the trade name for a range of specialist needlework material which includes an excellent even-weave fabric (known as Article 429) made of cotton and Modal. It is easy to wash and iron and is an ideal medium for counted needlework. It is woven in single threads rather than blocks (similar to linen) and is available in over forty colours.

Linen Bands

There are a number of banded products on the market in Aida, Hardanger and linen. The bands used in this book all come from mainland Europe in a variety of widths, styles and colours, sometimes with decorative edges added in cotton.

Zweigart Linda

This material, similar to linen in appearance but made from a mixture of cotton and synthetics, is ideal for products which need to be easy-care, for instance, for baby and table linens.

Stitching Paper

This product is based as closely as possible on the early Victorian punched paper. The original perforated or punched paper was made in England, possibly as early as 1840. Early examples of the stitching paper were bought as small decorated circles or squares and were used to decorate empty spaces in scrap books. The Victorians loved working on the paper and produced bookmarks, needlecases, pincushions, glove and handkerchief boxes, notebook covers and greeting cards.

Stitching paper can be stitched, folded, glued and cut to make pretty cross-stitch projects as illustrated on page 107.

Hints for stitching on paper:
• Although the paper is quite strong, do remember it needs to be handled with care.
• There is a right and a wrong side to the paper, the smoother side being the right side.
• Avoid folding the paper unless this is part of the design.
• Find the centre with a ruler and mark with a pencil. Pencil lines can be removed with a soft rubber.
• Use three strands of embroidery cotton for the

cross-stitch and one or two strands for outlining.

• Work any outlining in back-stitch after the cross-stitch is complete.

• When stitching is complete, cut out the design using the cutting line (if shown) as a guide or leaving one complete square around the stitching.

• Double-sided designs like the bookmark on page 107 can be fixed together using a little double-sided tape.

Threads

For all the projects in this book I have selected DMC stranded cotton (floss) for the cross-stitch although the colour keys on the charts indicate an alternative Anchor shade number where possible. Where alternative Anchor numbers are quoted an exact colour match is not always possible.

Stranded cotton is a six-ply mercerized cotton which is usually divided before stitching. At the beginning of each section in the stitching notes, I have indicated how many strands of stranded cotton are used in the example shown in the colour picture. If you alter the fabric selection for a particular project, remember to check the number of threads needed for that fabric.

If you are stitching on linen and you are not sure of the number of strands needed for the cross-stitch, the best way is to carefully pull out a thread of the fabric and compare this with your chosen yarn. The thread(s) on your needle should be roughly the same weight as that of the fabric.

When selecting threads, always have the fabric you are intending to use close at hand because the colour of your background fabric will affect the choice of colours. When in a shop, check the colour of the thread in daylight as electric light can 'kill' some shades. It is possible to buy 'daylight' bulbs to use in normal spotlights at home – a great help when shading a design in the evening.

Organizing your threads

It really does pay to start with good habits if possible and have an organizer for your threads. There are many excellent organizer systems on the market, but I make my own organizer cards (see below). The card from inside a packet of stockings is excellent, but any stiff card will do. Punch holes down each side and take a skein of stranded cotton (floss). Cut the cotton into manageable lengths of about 80 cm (31.5 inches), double them and thread them through the holes as shown. It is quite simple to remove one length of thread from the card without disturbing the rest. Label the card with the manufacturer's name and shade number and when the project is complete, all the threads will be labelled ready for the next project.

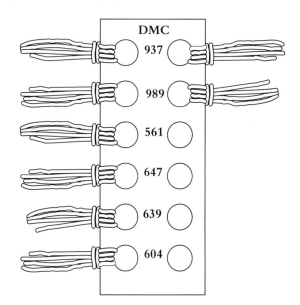

Make your own organizer

Needles

With all counted cross-stitch you will need blunt tapestry needles of various sizes depending on which fabric you choose. The most commonly used tapestry needles for cross-stitch are sizes 24 and 26. Avoid leaving your needle in the fabric when it is put away as it may leave a mark. The nickel plating on needles varies so much that some stitchers find their needles discolour and mark their hands and fabric. As a result they treat themselves to gold-plated needles which may be used again and again.

If you are not sure which needle to choose, it is possible to check in the following way. Push the needle through the fabric. It should pass through without enlarging the hole and fall through easily.

When beads are suggested in a project they may be attached using a fine sharp needle and a half cross-stitch. Beading needles are available but can be expensive if used rarely.

Frames and hoops

This subject always raises questions and argument. It is not necessary to use a frame or hoop for cross-stitch on linen or Aida. Having said that, it is a matter of personal choice and if you prefer to use one then please do so.

If you decide to use a rotating frame, these come in a variety of shapes and sizes and can be hand-held or free-standing. The needlework is stitched to the

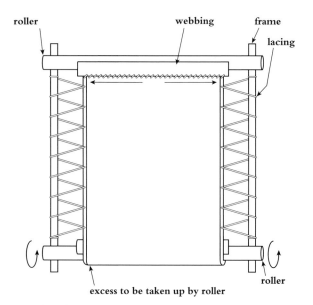

A rotating frame

webbing along the width of the frame and the excess material is taken up by rollers at the top and bottom (see diagram).

If you use a hoop, ensure that all the design is within the stitching area of the hoop and that you do not need to move the hoop across worked areas as this may drag and spoil your stitches.

Scissors

Keep a small, sharp pair of pointed scissors exclusively for your stitching. To avoid hunting for them down the side of the sofa, wear them around your neck on a ribbon!

Charts

The needlework charts in this book are illustrated in colour, some with a symbol to aid colour identification. Each square, both occupied and unoccupied, represents two threads of linen or one block of Aida, unless stated. Each occupied square equals one stitch. At this stage each stitch is presumed to be a complete cross-stitch.

What determines the size of a cross-stitch design is the number of stitches up and down and the thread count of the fabric. If you are familiar with knitting, it is similar to the difference in the size between the same number of stitches worked in 4-ply wool and in a chunky-weight wool.

Calculating design size

To calculate the design size, look at the chart and count the number of stitches in each direction. Divide this number by the number of stitches to 2.5 cm (1 inch) on the fabric of your choice and this will determine the completed design size. Always add a margin for stretching, framing or finishing.

I suggest adding 13 cm (5 inches) to both dimensions as a rule of thumb. For example, a design worked in 14-count Aida, which had 140 stitches across and 112 stitches down would give you:

140÷14= 25 cm (10 inches)

112÷14 = 20 cm (8 inches)

The design size would therefore be 25 x 20 cm (10 x 8 inches) and the stitch count 140 x 112.

I have included a stitch count for every design illustrated in the book. Before starting any of the counted projects in this book, it is vital to check the thread count of your chosen fabric and the stitch count of the chart you are intending to use and make sure that the design will fit. This is particularly important if the finished piece is intended to fit a special frame, trinket pot or card.

Planning Layout Charts

This section is included to help make the task of planning chart layouts much easier. This exercise is also necessary because it is not possible to include the charts in full for all the designs in this book. Some of the illustrated projects need to be planned before you start stitching.

I always use Chartwell graph paper with a light grey grid and a light, but not white, background. I usually use the Imperial version – 10 squares to 2.5 cm (1 inch) – to make counting squares easier.

It is not necessary to copy all the detail when planning layouts. The coloured charts in this book are drawn with a solid outline, which you may choose not to stitch but can be copied simply to mark the position of motifs within the overall design.

Decide on the completed size of the stitched project and select which fabric you intend to use. You should at least have the thread count even if you don't have the actual material. Mark on the graph paper with a soft pencil where the centre and

the extremes of the chart should appear. This becomes the master sheet.

Still using a soft pencil, copy the outlines of the motifs you have selected onto another piece of graph paper. If only one side of a border is illustrated, copy out one section and reverse using the window method as follows. Choose a window with a large pane of glass and carefully tape the drawing to the glass with the back of the drawing facing you. You will see that the design can be reversed and turned upside down and then traced onto your master sheet.

When you have copied all the motifs you require, it is quite simple to cut out each section and lay it in position on the master sheet. When you are satisfied with the layout you can begin stitching using the colour charts from the book.

How to do a cross-stitch

One cross-stitch has two parts and can be worked in one of two ways. A complete stitch can be worked or a number of half stitches may be stitched in one line and then completed on the return journey. The one essential rule is that all the top stitches must face the same direction.

For this example the cross-stitch is being worked on linen, over two threads of fabric, using two strands of stranded cotton (floss). When working counted stitches on a single-weave fabric like linen

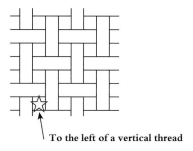

To the left of a vertical thread

Starting to the left of a vertical thread

or Jobelan, always start the stitching to the left of a vertical thread (see diagram) which appears as a larger, easier hole to see and acts as a warning if you have miscounted. You will always be in the same position on the fabric so if you have made a mistake, you will see it quickly.

Single cross-stitch showing position of needle

Bring the needle up through the wrong side of the fabric at the bottom left, cross two threads and insert in the top right. Push the needle through, then bring it up at the bottom right-hand corner, ready to complete the stitch in the top left-hand corner. To work the adjacent stitch, bring the needle up at the bottom right-hand corner of the first stitch (thus the stitches share points of entry and exit). To make part-completed stitches, work the first leg of the cross-stitch as above but, instead of completing the stitch, work the next half stitch and continue to the end of the row. The cross is completed on the return journey.

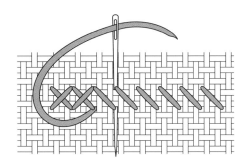

Part-completed stitches – completed on return journey

How to start

Knotless loop start

Having learned the basic cross-stitch, you now need to know how to start off using the knotless loop start. This method can be very useful with stranded cotton (floss), but it only works if you are intending to stitch with an even number of threads i.e. 2, 4 or 6. Cut the stranded cotton roughly twice the length you would normally need and carefully separate one strand. Double this thread and thread your needle with the two ends. Pierce your fabric from the wrong side where you intend to place your first stitch, leaving the looped end at the rear of the work. Return your needle to the wrong side after forming a half cross-stitch, and pass the needle through the waiting loop (see diagram). The stitch is anchored and you may begin to stitch.

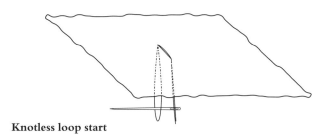

Knotless loop start

Away waste knot

When working with an uneven number of threads, start by anchoring the thread at the front of the work, away from and above the stitching area. This thread can be stitched in to the back of the work when stitches have been formed.

How to finish

When a group of stitches or a length of thread is completed, finish off the end carefully before starting a new colour. At the back of the work pass the needle under stitches of the same or similar colour and snip off the loose end close to the stitching. Small loose ends have a nasty habit of pulling through to the right side!

Where to start

It can be nerve-racking at the start when you are faced with a plain unprinted piece of fabric, but it is really very simple. The secret is to start in the middle of the fabric and in the middle of the chart, unless stated. Using this method there will always be enough fabric to stretch and frame. Always cut your fabric at least 13 cm (5 inches) larger than the intended completed dimensions. (See Calculating design size, page 20.)

To find the middle of the fabric, fold it into four and press lightly (see diagram). Open out and work a narrow line of tacking (basting) stitches following the threads to mark the fold and the centre. These stitches should removed when the work is completed.

Check you have all the colours you need and mount all the threads on a piece of card alongside its shade number. Sew a narrow hem or oversew the raw edges to prevent fraying. This can be removed on completion. Thread your needle with the required number of strands and you are ready to go.

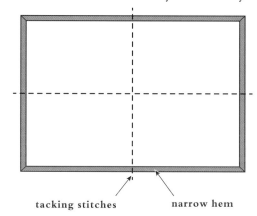

tacking stitches   narrow hem

Fold the fabric in four and tack along the folds

Back-stitch outlining

Outlining is the addition of a back-stitch outline to add detail or dimension to the picture. In all the charts in this book the solid lines surrounding the coloured symbols refer to a back-stitch outline and include a suggested DMC shade number. Outlining is very much an optional part of cross-stitch. It is not always necessary and is often a matter of taste (see Chrysanthemum Firescreen, page 64).

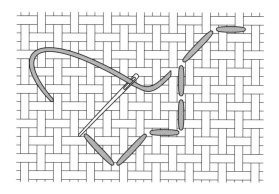

Back-stitch outlining

Tweeding

This is a simple way to increase the numbers of colours in your palette without buying more thread. To tweed, combine more than one coloured thread, put through the eye of the needle and work as one. You can apply this to working French knots and bullion bars to great effect.

Additional stitches

All the stitches in this book are used as counted stitches, although some of them are used in surface embroidery and crewel. It is often a way of adding a new dimension to a piece of cross-stitch (see Victorian Ladies, page 59).

Algerian eye

A pretty star-shaped stitch which may be added to cross-stitch with great effect. The stitch occupies the space taken by four cross-stitches and is worked in such a way that a small hole is formed.

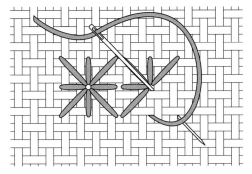

Algerian eye

Bullion bars

These unusual stitches can be adapted to the length required and can look very effective (see the wigs on Victorian Ladies, page 59).

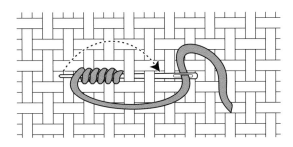

Bullion bars

Double cross-stitch

The double cross-stitch in this book has been worked over four threads. Work a cross-stitch first then add a vertical cross on top. Keep the direction of the stitch uniform.

Double cross-stitch

Drawn thread and somersault stitch

To form somersault stitch as illustrated in the diagram, you will need to remove some horizontal threads from the stitching area and re-weave them back into the border. Work the two lines of hem stitch as shown on the chart and then carefully snip the horizontal threads once. Unravel the thread and, using a needle, re-weave into the border section. Looking at the diagram, work the somersault stitches on the vertical threads left after re-weaving. I have used perle for the stitches in this book. You may like to try pure linen thread.

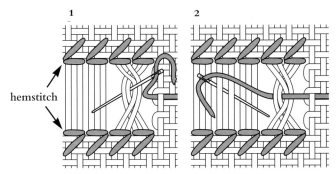

Somersault stitch combined with hemstitch

Four-sided stitch

This stitch is formed in straight lines on the right side of the fabric and diagonal lines on the back. This is a 'pulled' stitch which means that the thread is pulled firmly, thus forming the attractive holes as you stitch.

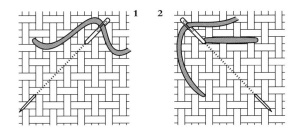

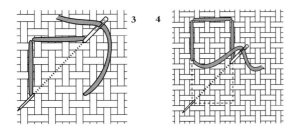

Four-sided stitch

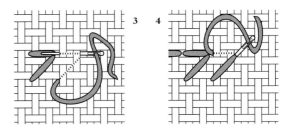

Hemstitch

French knots

French knots are useful little stitches and may be used in addition to cross-stitch. Bring the needle up to the right side of the fabric, wind the thread around the needle twice and 'post' the needle through to the back, one thread or part of a block away from the entry point. This stops the stitch pulling to the wrong side. If you want bigger knots, add more thread to the needle – this seems to give a better finish than winding more times. Random uncounted French knots are almost free embroidery without the panic and are great fun. I outline the area with a single line of back-stitch and then pack in the French knots until the area is completely covered (see the wigs on the Lovers Sampler, page 68).

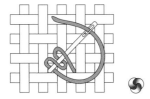

French knot

Hemstitch

A simple two-part stitch which anchors the threads before any are withdrawn.

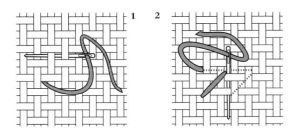

Herringbone stitch

A useful and decorative stitch used on band samplers (see Traditional Band Sampler, page 137).

Herringbone stitch

Hollie point stitch

This pretty stitch is formed on the front of the fabric, the needle not piercing the material. The area is outlined in back stitch first, then horizontal threads are laid across the surface. The lace-like stitch is formed on these horizontal threads.

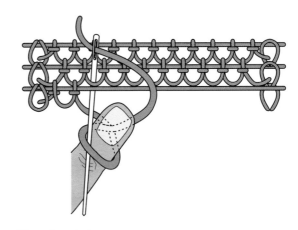

Hollie point stitch

Long-legged cross-stitch

This stitch covers two threads of linen and is worked from left to right, giving a braided effect.

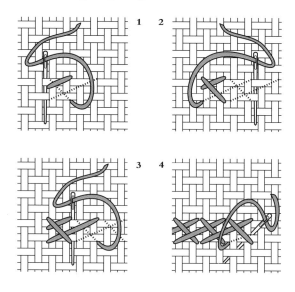

Long-legged cross-stitch

Queen stitch

This lovely ancient stitch is made of four parts and forms little dimples in the embroidery.

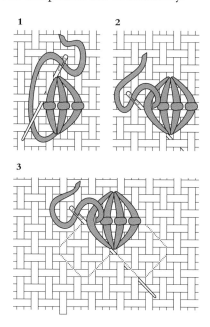

Queen stitch

Satin stitch

A long smooth stitch which covers the fabric. You may need to experiment with the number of strands of stranded cotton needed to achieve the desired effect.

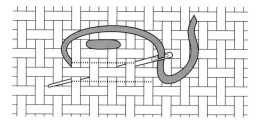

Satin stitch

Three-quarter stitch

An easy way to form a triangle using part cross-stitch. This helps to remove the 'step' effect.

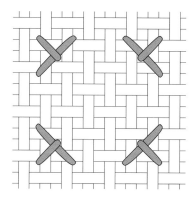

Three-quarter stitch

The Treasures

Amish Quilt

This chapter was inspired, and I mean inspired, by looking at an Amish quilt while visiting America recently. I was amazed by the beauty and the simplicity of the patterns in the quilts using what I can only describe as an explosion of colour in the patchwork and the perfection of the tiny quilting stitches. The Amish community, hardly touched by modern inventions and one in which crime and divorce are almost unheard of, has doubled its size in the last twenty years. The Amish originally had their roots in the Protestant Reformation and survived as part of the Mennonite communities in Germany, France and Holland. The name 'Amish' is derived from a Mennonite minister, Jakob Amman, who believed that the established church was too relaxed on matters of discipline and religion, and advocated family unity strengthened by separation from worldliness. The Amish life, dominated by faith and family, is thriving today and their magnificent quilts and coverlets are made in the same traditional styles as during the last century.

I have linked the four Amish patterns using the theme of the four seasons and the finished panels are combined to make the decorative floor cushion illustrated overleaf. Each panel is drawn to the same stitch count and made up in identical fashion, so I have only included one set of instructions.

Four Seasons Floor Cushion

Skill level 1

Stitch count: 121 x 121
Design size: 21.5 cm (8.5 inches) square
Stitching notes: suitable for Aida or even-weave. Use two strands of stranded cotton (floss) for the cross-stitch and one strand for the optional outlines. The star pattern includes a number of three-quarter stitches, but you will see from the colour photograph that these can be worked successfully on Aida, with care, and using the softer (less 'dressed') versions of this fabric.

You Will Need

33 cm (13 inches) square beige Aida, 14 blocks to
  2.5 cm (1 inch)
Stranded cottons (floss) as listed on the chart

Instructions

Work a narrow hem around the edge to prevent fraying. Fold into four, press lightly and mark the folds with a line of tacking (basting) stitches.

Starting at the centre of the design, begin to stitch using two strands of stranded cotton for the cross-stitch and working over one block. Remember to keep the top stitch facing the same way and finish off the loose ends as you stitch by putting the needle to the back of the work and under stitches of the same or similar colour. Snip off the loose ends close to the stitching. Add the optional back-stitch, referring to the chart for suggested shade numbers.

When the stitching is complete, check for missed stitches and press lightly on the wrong side (see page 148). Set aside until all four panels are completed and make up as described on page 150.

Pinwheel

This pinwheel design is inspired by the windmills which provide the energy to pump water to the fields and houses. It reminds me of the daffodils which line the lanes near our home in the Cotswolds.

Carolina lily

This lily is an unusual subject for an Amish quilt because it is forbidden to copy objects from nature (the reproduction of graven images), but this very stylized flower does occur. I have used strong 'hot' colours to give the panel a summery feel.

Baskets

This appealing motif is a familiar country or folk design and regularly appears on Amish quilts. Baskets are an integral part of the rural life of the Amish as the produce from the fields has to be moved to market and then to home. I chose this pattern for the autumn colourway, reminded of baskets of windfall apples under our apple tree and of brambles picked and ready to freeze.

Stars

Stars, and in fact all the heavenly bodies, are used as motifs in Amish quilt-making. The Amish communities do not use electricity and rely on gas lamps to light their activities in the evening. The view of the sky, uninterrupted by street lamps, must surely inspire some of these dramatic patterns. As mentioned in the introduction, this design includes a number of three-quarter stitches which require a little extra attention when stitched on Aida. If you are not familiar with this stitch, please refer to Additional stitches on page 26.

Amish Picture Panels

If you prefer, these four designs would make four striking individual framed pictures, hung together in a group. I have worked the designs on beige Aida fabric but you could select four different coloured materials, for example, Jobelan even weave. If you intend to hang pictures in a group, check that you stitch all the designs on fabric with the same count.

The Amish patterns Pinwheel, Carolina Lily, Baskets, and Stars inspired this fun project.

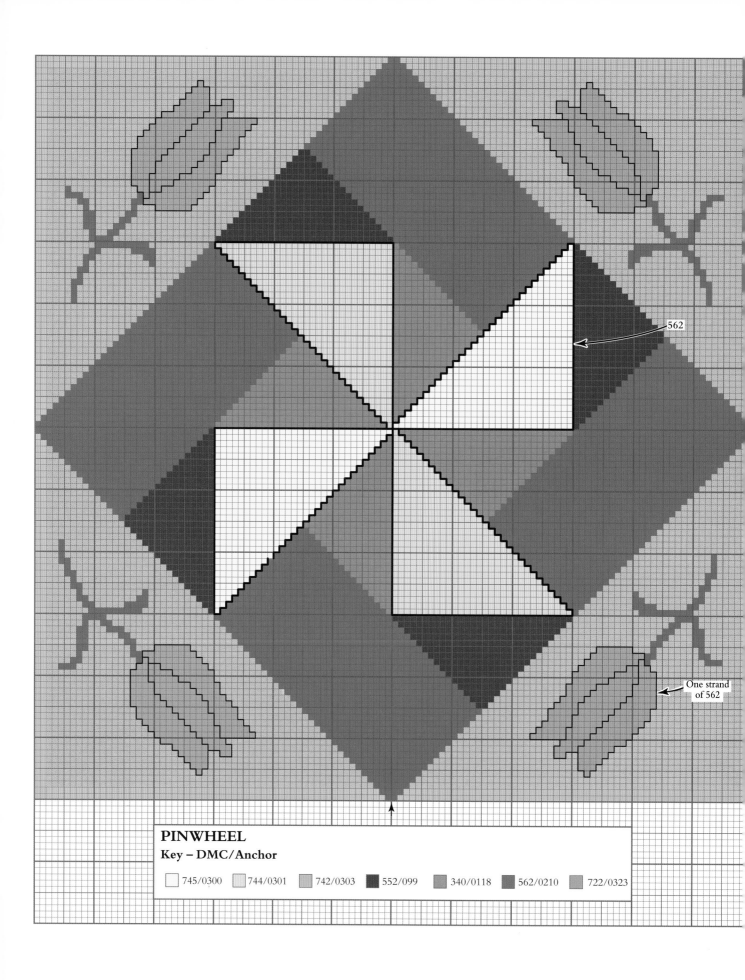

562

One strand of 562

PINWHEEL
Key – DMC/Anchor

745/0300   744/0301   742/0303   552/099   340/0118   562/0210   722/0323

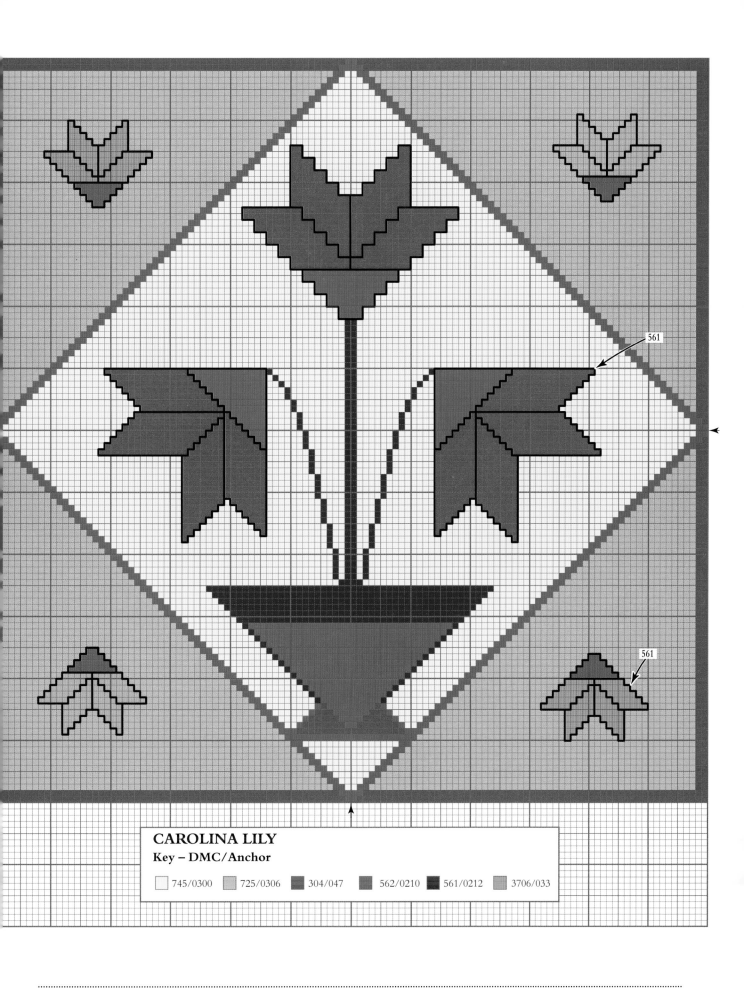

CAROLINA LILY
Key – DMC/Anchor

745/0300	725/0306	304/047	562/0210	561/0212	3706/033

561

561

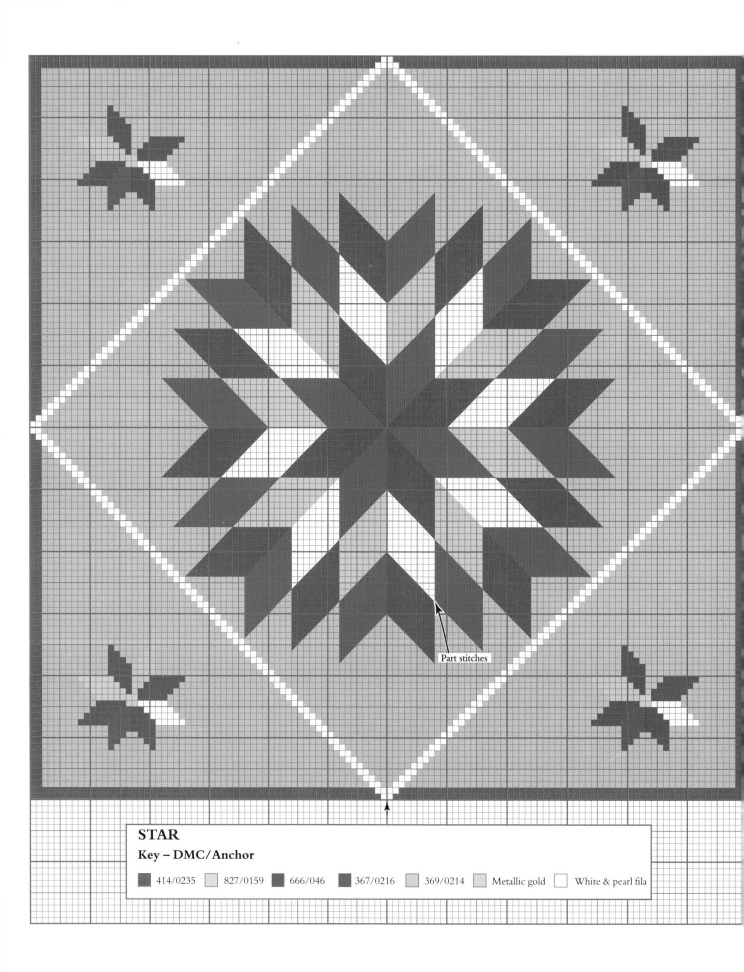

Part stitches

STAR
Key – DMC/Anchor

■ 414/0235	☐ 827/0159	■ 666/046	■ 367/0216	☐ 369/0214	☐ Metallic gold	☐ White & pearl fila

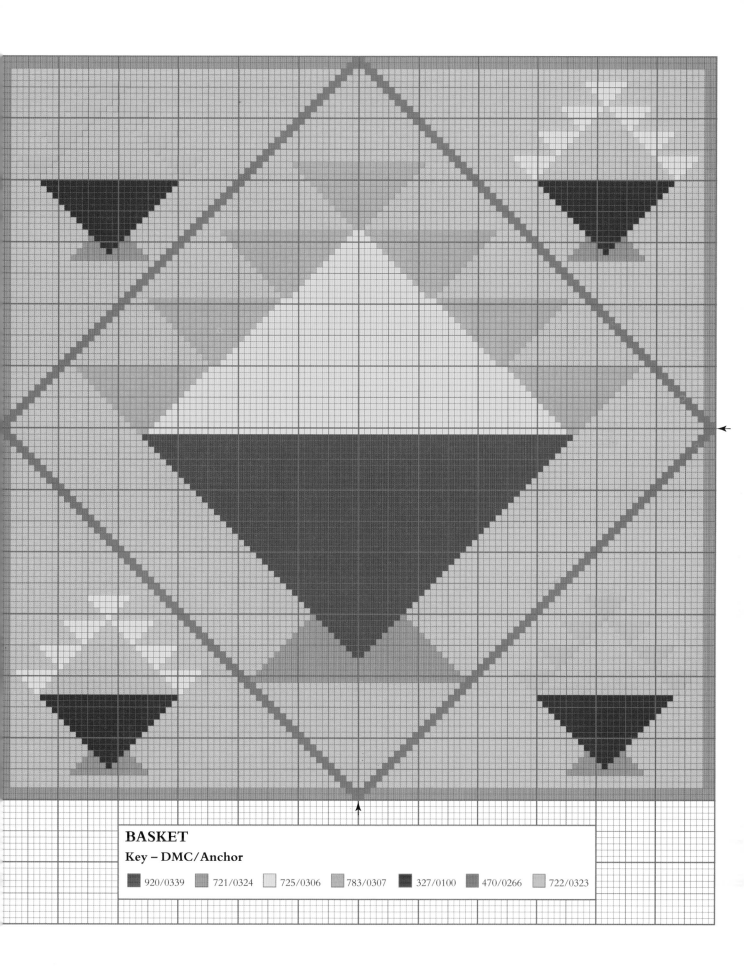

BASKET

Key – DMC/Anchor

920/0339 721/0324 725/0306 783/0307 327/0100 470/0266 722/0323

Spot Motif Sampler

This unusual piece of embroidery is based on two 'spot' samplers seen on my numerous visits to The Burrell Collection in Glasgow, which always leaves me inspired. Random pattern or motif samplers were commonly stitched during the seventeenth century in Britain, partly as a record of stitches and patterns and also as pieces of appliqué. A design would be stitched on one piece of fabric and kept until needed; in some cases it was then cut out and applied to a garment or piece of furnishing.

Random Motif Sampler

Skill level 5

Stitch count: 183 x 215

Design size: 32 x 38 cm (12.5 x 15 inches)

Stitching notes: not suitable for Aida; use even-weave. Two strands of stranded cotton (floss) for the cross-stitch, Algerian eye and queen stitch and one strand for back-stitch outlines.

YOU WILL NEED

44.5 x 50.5 cm (17.5 x 20 inches) mid-beige Jobelan 27/28 threads to 2.5 cm (1 inch)

Stranded cottons (floss) as listed on the chart

Graph paper and soft pencil

INSTRUCTIONS

Work a narrow hem around the edge of the linen to prevent fraying. Fold into four, press lightly and, starting to the right of a vertical thread (see How to do a cross-stitch, page 21), mark the folds with a line of tacking (basting) stitches. Set aside.

PLANNING A LAYOUT CHART

Before beginning this project you will need to plan the position of each motif on graph paper (refer to Planning layout charts, page 21). The charts on pages 38-40 include all the motifs and patterns for the exquisite picture illustrated opposite. It is not necessary to copy all the detail from the charts – use the outline only. The stitching can be worked from the colour charts when you have planned the correct motif positions. If you wish to alter the letter 'A' motifs, select an initial from the Random Letter Sampler on page 72 and add to your chart.

When you are satisfied with your layout chart start at the centre and to the left of a vertical thread and begin to stitch, using two strands of stranded cotton for the cross-stitch. Remember to keep the top stitch facing the same way and finish off the loose ends as you stitch.

The strawberry motifs illustrated in the picture opposite are then stitched in queen stitch (see Additional stitches, page 26) but in cross-stitch on the Strawberry Pincushion and Scissor-keeper shown on page 43. Work the lace motif in cross-stitch and back-stitch, adding the Algerian eye

This charming sampler includes cross-stitch and Algerian eye. These attractive motifs may be used separately to fill cards or trinket pots or added to other projects in the book.

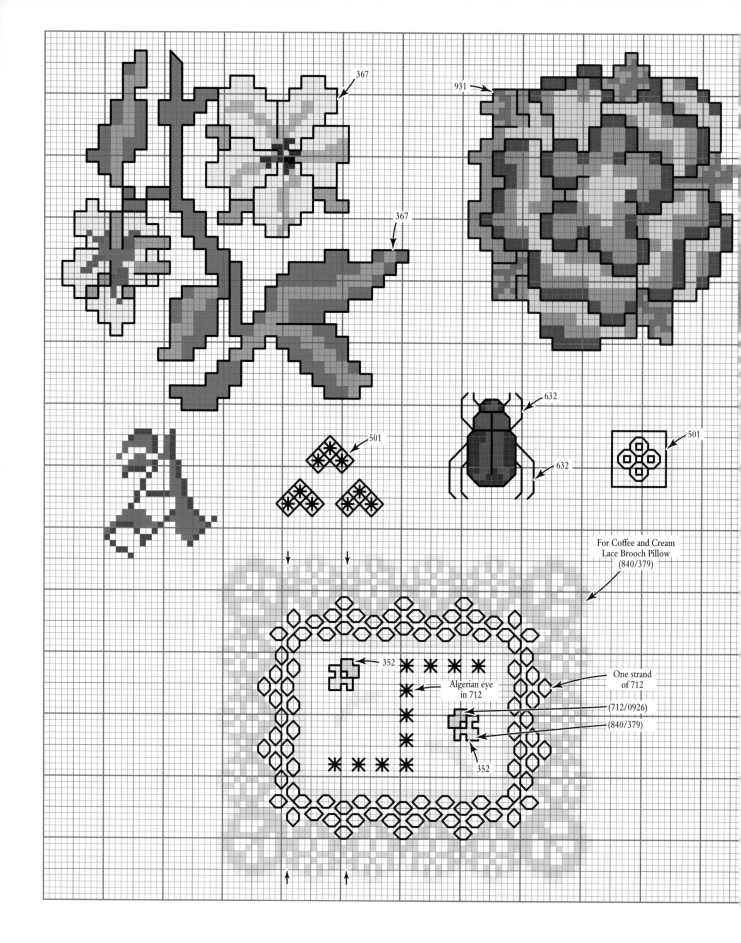

367

931

367

632

632

501

501

For Coffee and Cream
Lace Brooch Pillow
(840/379)

352

Algerian eye
in 712

One strand
of 712

(712/0926)

(840/379)

352

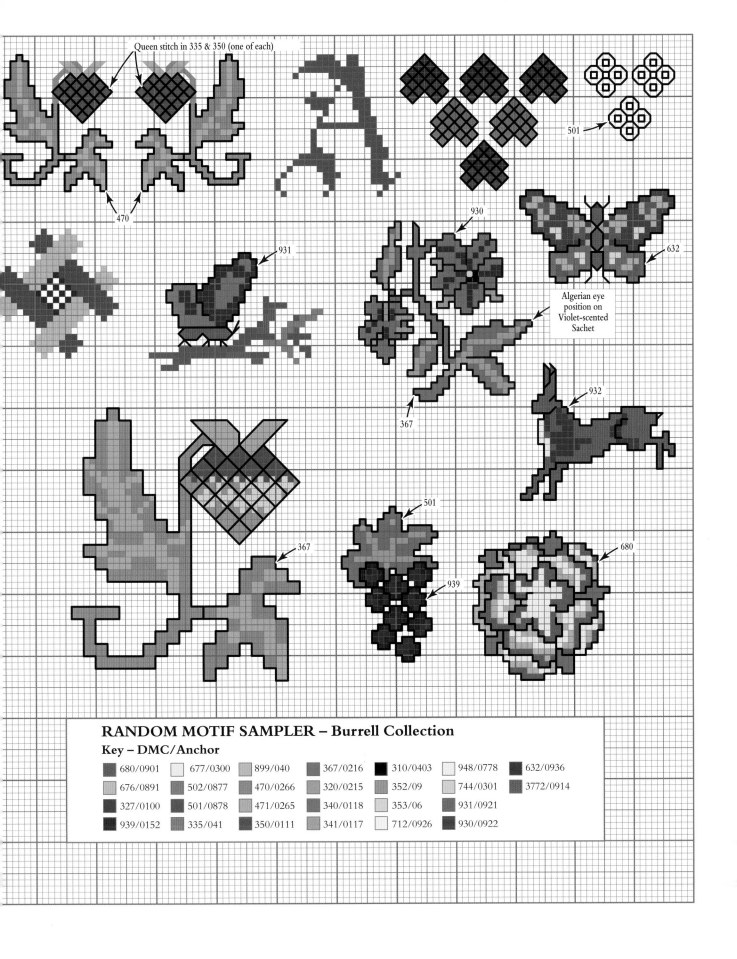

Queen stitch in 335 & 350 (one of each)

501

470

931

930

632

Algerian eye
position on
Violet-scented
Sachet

367

932

367

501

939

680

RANDOM MOTIF SAMPLER – Burrell Collection
Key – DMC/Anchor

680/0901	677/0300	899/040	367/0216	310/0403	948/0778	632/0936
676/0891	502/0877	470/0266	320/0215	352/09	744/0301	3772/0914
327/0100	501/0878	471/0265	340/0118	353/06	931/0921	
939/0152	335/041	350/0111	341/0117	712/0926	930/0922	

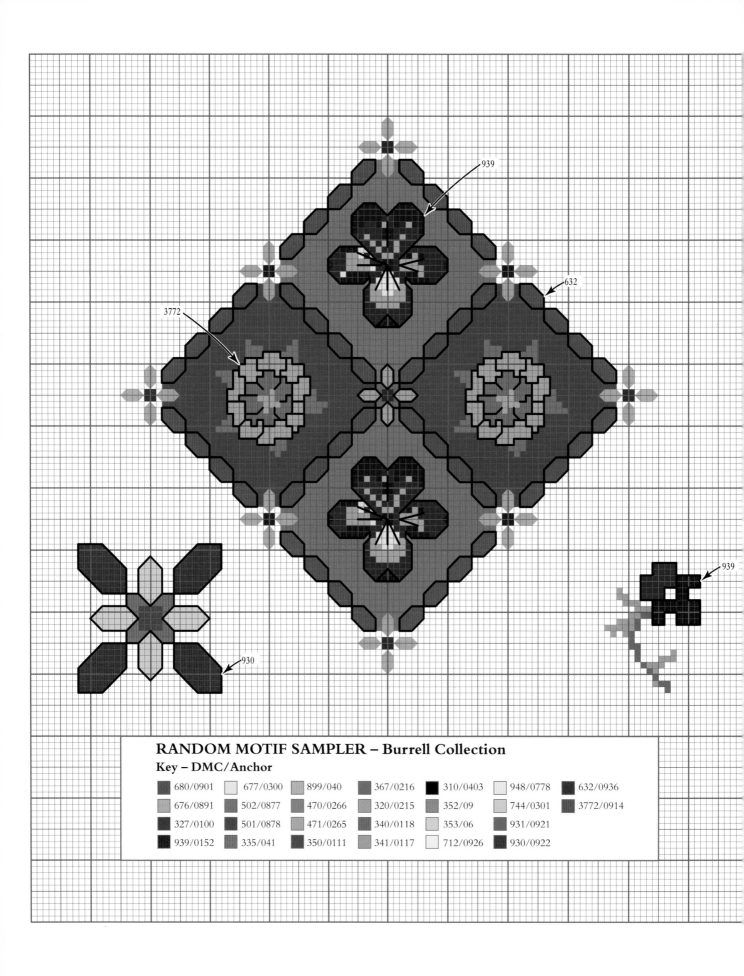

RANDOM MOTIF SAMPLER – Burrell Collection
Key – DMC/Anchor

680/0901	677/0300	899/040	367/0216	310/0403	948/0778	632/0936
676/0891	502/0877	470/0266	320/0215	352/09	744/0301	3772/0914
327/0100	501/0878	471/0265	340/0118	353/06	931/0921	
939/0152	335/041	350/0111	341/0117	712/0926	930/0922	

stitches in the centre and taking care to keep the hole at the centre of the stitch free of loose ends (see Additional stitches, page 24). Try to avoid carrying threads across unstitched areas as they will show through to the right side when the design is stretched and framed. Add the optional back-stitch outline, referring to the suggested shade numbers on the chart.

When complete, check for missed stitches, press on the wrong side and mount and frame as preferred.

Coffee and Cream Lace Brooch Pillow

This pretty project has been adapted from the lace panel on the Spot Motif Sampler, although I have omitted one small pattern repeat to obtain a square design, adapted the colours slightly and added a few small seed pearls. The antique lace was a lucky find though I have achieved similar effects dipping lace in weak tea (see Ageing linen, page 148)!

Skill Level 3
Stitch count: 53 x 53
Design size: 9.5 cm (3.75 inches) square (not including silk border)
Stitching notes: suitable for Aida and even-weave. Use two strands of stranded cotton (floss) for the cross-stitch (altered colourway shown in brackets on the chart) and one strand for the back-stitch. Seed pearls are added with half cross-stitch.

You Will Need
20 cm (8 inches) square tea-dyed linen, 25 threads to 2.5 cm (1 inch)
Stranded cottons (floss) as listed in brackets on the chart
2 m (2.2 yards) antique cream or tea-dyed lace
30 Mill Hill seed pearls
Beading needle or sharp, size 10 needle

Cream silk to complete the cushion (see Making inset cushions, page 148)

Instructions
Work a narrow hem around the edge of the linen to prevent fraying. Fold into four, press lightly and, starting to the right of a vertical thread (see Where to start, page 23), mark the folds with a line of tacking (basting) stitches. If working the design from the colour chart on page 38, start in the middle and work the design remembering to keep the top stitch facing the same direction. If you wish to produce a square design as shown in the illustration, omit one scallop pattern around the border (indicated by two small arrows on the chart).

When the cross-stitch is complete, add the seed

The lace panel is inset into cream silk cushion and I have used it to keep brooches and hat pins safe, but it would also make a lovely wedding ring pillow.

pearls (optional) using a beading needle or sharp needle and one strand of stranded cotton that blends with the background. Check for missed stitches, press lightly (see page 148) and make up as described on page 148.

Violet-scented Sachet

The illustrated scented sachet is full of violet pot pourri, but would make an equally lovely gift full of lavender, tiny perfumed soaps or bath crystals. The top of the sachet is closed with a pretty ribbon to which you could add some tiny fabric flowers to match the stitching.

Skill Level 3
Stitch count: 54 x 54
Design size: 10 x 10 cm (4 x 4 inches)
Stitching notes: suitable for Aida and even-weave. Use two strands of stranded cotton (floss) for the cross-stitch and Algerian eye and one strand for the back-stitch.

YOU WILL NEED
16.5 cm (6.5 inches) square buttermilk Jobelan, 27/28 threads to 2.5 cm (1 inch)
Stranded cottons (floss) as listed on the chart
Cream lace to trim (optional)

INSTRUCTIONS
Work a narrow hem around the edge of the linen to prevent fraying. Fold into four, press lightly and, starting to the right of a vertical thread (see Where to start, page 23), mark the folds with a line of tacking (basting) stitches. Set aside.

Starting in the middle of the fabric and to the left of a vertical thread, work the cross-stitch keeping the top stitch facing the same direction. Add the back-stitch outline, referring to the chart for suggested shade numbers.

An exquisite project to give as a gift, the cross-stitch violets are surrounded by rows of Algerian eye stitches to add a lacy effect, trimmed with lace, tied with gold ribbon and filled with scented pot pourri or tiny soaps.

To work the lacy border of Algerian eye stitches (see Additional stitches, page 24), count out from the leaf (marked on the chart with an arrow) four threads (or two blocks if working on Aida) and work Algerian eye stitches alternately as illustrated.

If you are unfamiliar with the Algerian eye stitches, practise in the margin of the fabric. The secret is always to pass the needle down through the centre of the stitch and remember that it is a 'pulled' stitch. This is the one time when you are allowed to make the holes in the fabric larger than they were intended! It is this technique which forms the neat round hole in the centre of the stitch, which should be free of any threads at the back of the work.

When stitching is complete check for missed stitches, press lightly and make up as described on page 151.

Strawberry Pincushion and Scissor-keeper

These pretty, useful projects are worked by simply reversing the large strawberry motif illustrated at the bottom right of the Random Motif Sampler, and adapting the leaves to fit on the scissor-keeper. The fruit is worked in cross-stitch instead of queen stitch as illustrated in the main project. The Liberty lawn material used to make up the pincushion and trim the scissor-keeper is based on a special colourway of the William Morris design known as the Strawberry Thief. The new colourway was specifically designed to celebrate the centenary of the designer's death in 1996.

These useful needlework accessories are stitched on blue Jobelan and trimmed with Liberty lawn. The lawn design is the Strawberry Thief designed originally by William Morris and is available in many colourways.

Pincushion

Skill Level 2
Stitch count: 27 x 30

Design size: 5 x 5.5 cm (2 x 2.25 inches)

Stitching notes: suitable for Aida or even-weave fabric. Two strands of stranded cotton (floss) for the cross-stitch and one strand for the optional back-stitch outline. If you decide to work the motifs in queen stitch as on the Random Motif Sampler, you must use an even-weave fabric and not Aida.

YOU WILL NEED

11.5 x 12.5 cm (4.5 x 5 inches) denim blue Jobelan, 28 threads to 2.5 cm (1 inch)

Stranded cottons (floss) as listed on the chart

25.5 cm (10 inches) Liberty lawn (Strawberry Thief)

INSTRUCTIONS

Work a narrow hem around the edge of the linen to prevent fraying. Fold into four, press lightly and, starting to the right of a vertical thread (see How to do a cross-stitch, page 21), mark the folds with a line of tacking (basting) stitches. Set aside. Starting in the middle and to the left of a vertical thread, work the cross-stitch keeping the top stitch facing the same direction. Add the back-stitch outline, referring to the chart for suggested shade numbers.

When the cross-stitch is complete, make up as inset cushion as described on page 148.

Scissor-keeper

Skill Level 2

Stitch count: 20 x 20

Design size: 4 cm (1.5 inches) square

Stitching notes: suitable for Aida or even-weave fabric. Two strands of stranded cotton (floss) for the cross-stitch and one strand for the optional back-stitch outline.

YOU WILL NEED

7.5 cm (3 inches) square denim blue Jobelan, 28 threads to 2.5 cm (1 inch)

Stranded cottons (floss) as listed on the chart

10 cm (4 inches) square Liberty lawn (Strawberry Thief)

INSTRUCTIONS

Work a narrow hem around the edge of the linen to prevent fraying. Fold in four, press lightly and, starting to the right of a vertical thread (see How to do a cross-stitch, page 21), mark the folds with a line of tacking (basting) stitches.

Starting in the middle and to the left of a vertical thread, work the cross-stitch keeping the top stitch facing the same direction. Add the back-stitch outline, referring to the chart for suggested shade numbers. Check for missed stitches and press on the wrong side (see page 148). Make up as described on page 150.

Dutch Motif Sampler

This is a personal favourite of mine based on two stunning samplers seen at the City Museum in Rotterdam, Holland. The wonderful mixture of random motifs, repeating patterns, flowers and animals always arouses the creative instinct in me and here are just some of the results.

Braided Sampler Cushion

Skill Level 3

Stitch count: 209 x 209

Design size: 38 x 38 cm (15 x 15 inches)

Stitching notes: suitable for even-weave fabric. Use two strands of stranded cotton (floss) for the cross-stitch and queen stitch and one strand for the back-stitch.

You Will Need

2 x 50 cm (20 inches) square pieces of 'boiled' or tea-dyed linen, 28 threads to 2.5 cm (1 inch)

Stranded cottons (floss) as listed on the chart

4 tassels (purchased)

Appleton crewel wool in shade numbers 223, 545, 606, 695, 253 and 925 to make twisted braid

Instructions

Work a narrow hem around the edge of the linen to prevent fraying. Fold into four, press lightly and starting to the right of a vertical thread (see How to do a cross-stitch, page 21), mark the folds with a line of tacking (basting) stitches.

Starting at the centre of the design to the left of a vertical thread, begin to stitch using two strands of stranded cotton for the cross-stitch. Remember to keep the top stitch facing the same way. To finish off

the loose ends put the needle to the back of the work and under stitches of the same or similar colour. Snip off the loose ends close to the stitching.

Add the Algerian eye stitches, bearing in mind that it is a 'pulled' stitch and that the working thread should not be visible through the small hole at the centre of the stitch (see Additional stitches on page 24).

The queen stitches used for the pretty arrowhead motifs in the top corners of the cushion are also pulled stitches, forming small dimples in the pattern.

Add the optional back-stitch when the cross-stitch is complete, press on the wrong side and make up as described on page 148.

Black Motif Sampler

I have altered the colour of some of the motifs in this design to suit the black background and these are indicated on the chart in brackets. I have also included some small gold-coloured charms to the completed picture.

Skill Level 3

Stitch count: 149 x 149

Design size: 25.5 cm (10 x 10 inches) square

Stitching notes: suitable for Aida and even-weave.

Use two strands of stranded cotton (floss) for the cross-stitch and one strand for the back-stitch.

YOU WILL NEED

38 cm (15 inches) square black linen, 30 threads to 2.5 cm (1 inch)
Stranded cottons (floss) as listed on the chart (altered colours on chart)
Graph paper
Soft pencil
2 gold-coloured charms

INSTRUCTIONS

Work a narrow hem around the edge of the linen to prevent fraying. Fold into four, press lightly and, starting to the right of a vertical thread (see Where to start, page 23), mark the folds with a line of tacking (basting) stitches. Set aside.

PLANNING A LAYOUT CHART

Before beginning this project, you will need to select the motifs you like and plan the position on the graph paper (refer to Planning layout charts, page 21). Remember that it is not necessary to copy all the detail from the charts – use the outline only. The stitching can be worked from the colour charts when you have planned the correct motif positions.

When you are satisfied with your layout chart, start at the centre and to the left of a vertical thread and begin to stitch using two strands of stranded cotton for the cross-stitch. Remember to keep the top stitch facing the same way and finish off the loose ends as you stitch. Add the optional gold charms with a half cross-stitch and matching thread.

....

These two projects illustrate the remarkable effect achieved by changing the background colour of a design. The Braided Sampler Cushion is worked on linen and the Black Motif Sampler is stitched on black Jobelan. I have added purchased tassels and a hand-made cord to the cushion, and gilt charms to the picture.

When the stitching is complete, press lightly on the wrong side and frame as preferred (see page 156).

Diamond pincushion

....

Skill Level 2
Stitch count: 35 x 35
Design size: 9 x 9 cm (3.5 inches)
Stitching notes: suitable for Aida or even-weave. Use three strands of stranded cotton (floss) for the cross-stitch over two threads on linen.

A stunning repeating pattern added to a hard-wood pincushion. This pattern could be extended to fit a larger project, a footstool perhaps.

....

YOU WILL NEED

19 cm (7.5 inches) square unbleached linen, 20 threads to 2.5 cm (1 inch)
Stranded cottons (floss) as listed on the chart
1 dark-stained wooden pincushion base and pad

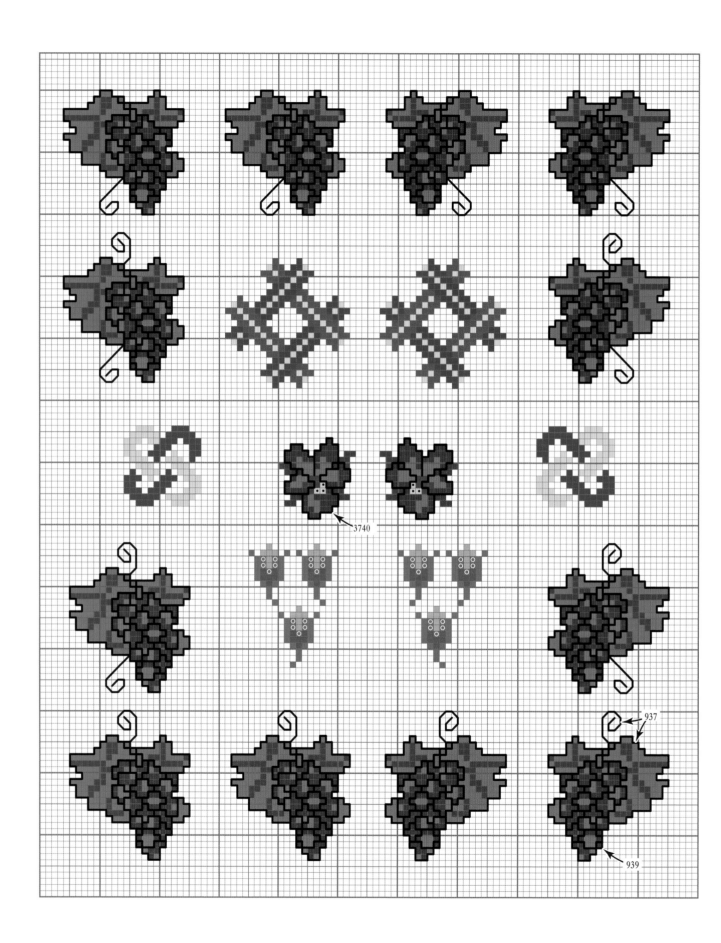

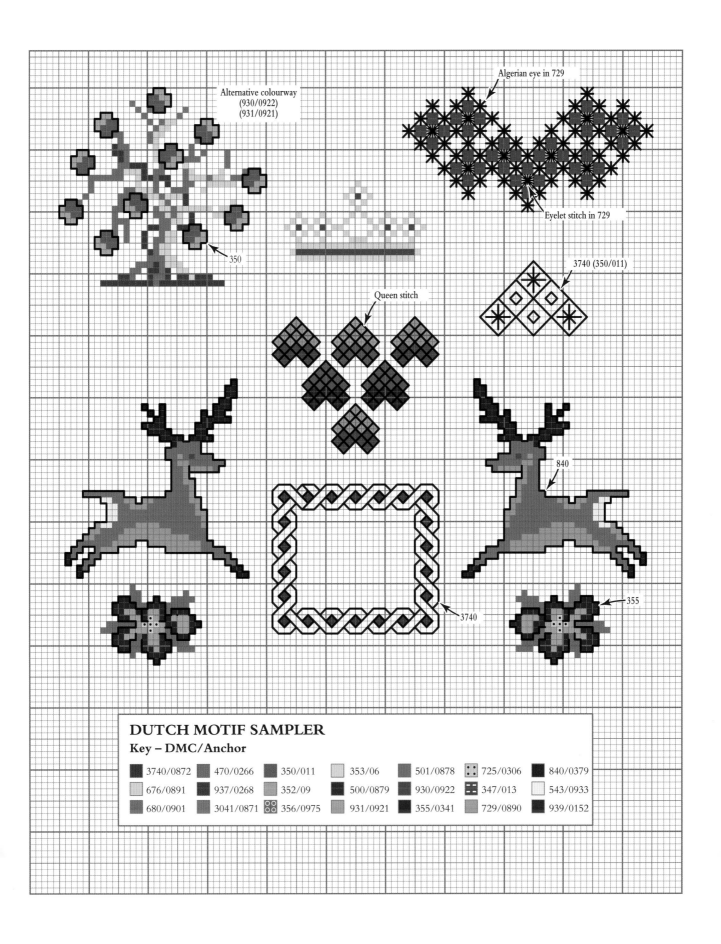

Alternative colourway
(930/0922)
(931/0921)

Algerian eye in 729

Eyelet stitch in 729

350

3740 (350/011)

Queen stitch

840

355

3740

DUTCH MOTIF SAMPLER
Key – DMC/Anchor

3740/0872	470/0266	350/011	353/06	501/0878	725/0306	840/0379
676/0891	937/0268	352/09	500/0879	930/0922	347/013	543/0933
680/0901	3041/0871	356/0975	931/0921	355/0341	729/0890	939/0152

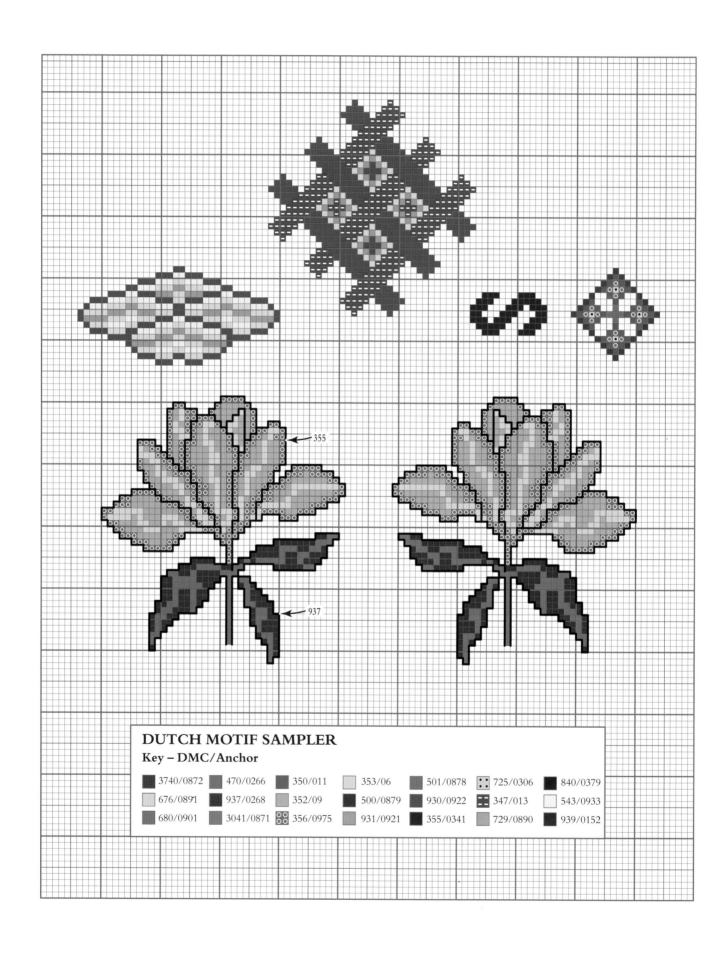

DUTCH MOTIF SAMPLER
Key – DMC/Anchor

■ 3740/0872	■ 470/0266	■ 350/011	☐ 353/06	■ 501/0878	⊡ 725/0306	■ 840/0379
▦ 676/0891	■ 937/0268	■ 352/09	■ 500/0879	■ 930/0922	⊟ 347/013	☐ 543/0933
■ 680/0901	■ 3041/0871	⊙ 356/0975	■ 931/0921	■ 355/0341	■ 729/0890	■ 939/0152

Work a narrow hem around the edge of the linen to prevent fraying. This is particularly important when using loose-weave linen as it really will fray! Fold into four, press lightly and, starting to the right of a vertical thread (see Where to start, page 23), mark the folds with a line of tacking (basting) stitches.

Working from the chart on page 50, start in the middle and to the left of a vertical thread and begin to stitch using two strands of stranded cotton for the cross-stitch. Remember to keep the top stitch facing the same way. At the back of the work, put the needle under stitches in the same or similar colour and snip off the loose ends close to the stitching.

When the cross-stitch is complete, check for missed stitches and press on the wrong side (see page 148). Make up as described on page 154.

Fruit Tree Needlecase

This appealing needlecase is stitched using the chart on page 49, with a simple border worked in two rows of long-legged cross-stitch. I have added initials and dates to personalize the project.

Skill Level 2
Stitch count: 53 x 44
Design size: 9.5 x 7.5 cm (3.75 x 3 inches)
Stitching notes: suitable for Aida and even-weave. Use two strands of stranded cotton (floss) for the cross-stitch and one strand for the back-stitch.

YOU WILL NEED
18 x 24 cm (7 x 9.5 inches) rich blue Jobelan shade
  61, 28 threads to 2.5 cm (1 inch)
Stranded cottons (floss) as listed on the chart
18 x 24 cm (7 x 9.5 inches) blue lining fabric
2 pieces 15 x 9 cm (6 x 3.5 inches) of flannel for
  needles

This useful needlework accessory is worked on blue Jobelan and includes a home-made cord and tassel. The tree motif is taken from the Braided Sampler Cushion and a personal touch added with the addition of initials.

INSTRUCTIONS
Work a narrow hem around the edge of the linen to prevent fraying. Lay the fabric on a clean flat surface, long side towards you. Fold in half, fold the top section in four and make the folds with tacking threads. This will be the front section of the needlecase. Press lightly and, starting to the right of a vertical thread (see How to do a cross-stitch, page 22), mark the folds with a line of tacking (basting) stitches.

Find the centre of the tree motif on the chart on page 49 and, starting to the left of a vertical thread, begin to stitch using two strands of stranded cotton for the cross-stitch. Remember to keep the top stitch facing the same way. Finish off the loose ends by taking the needle to the back of the work and putting it under stitches of the same or similar colour. Snip the loose ends close to the stitching.

If you wish to add initials to the design, select from either the Random Letter Sampler on page 72

or the Band Sampler on page 137. After the cross-stitch is complete, add the optional border of long-legged cross-stitch (see Additional stitches, page 26) and make a twisted cord to keep the flannel pages in place. For making up instructions, refer to page 152.

Purple Grape Picture Frame

Skill Level 2

Stitch count: 74 x 78
Design size: 14 cm (5.5 inches) square
Stitching notes: suitable for Aida and even-weave. Use two strands of stranded cotton (floss) for the cross-stitch and one strand for the back-stitch.

You Will Need

25.5 cm (10 inches) square Yorkshire Aida,
  14 blocks to 2.5 cm (1 inch)
Stranded cottons (floss) as listed on the chart
Graph paper
Soft pencil

Instructions

Work a narrow hem around the edge of the fabric to prevent fraying. Fold into four, press lightly and mark the folds with a line of tacking (basting) stitches. Set aside.

Planning A Layout Chart

Before beginning this project, you will need to plan the position of each grape motif on graph paper (refer to Planning layout charts, page 21). It is not necessary to copy all the detail from the charts but use the outline only. The stitching can be worked from the colour charts once you have planned the correct motif positions.

When you are satisfied with your layout chart, count from the centre of the fabric and begin to stitch using two strands of stranded cotton for the cross-stitch and working over one block of Aida. Remember to keep the top stitch facing the same way. Finish off the loose ends by taking the needle to the back of the work and putting the needle under stitches of the same or similar colour. Snip loose ends close to the stitching.

When the cross-stitch is complete add the back-stitch outline as preferred. Press lightly and make up as described in Finishing techniques on page 154.

A favourite photograph with a pretty decorated frame.

Navajo Woven Rug

This special project was inspired by my visit to Arizona and an ever-growing collection of Navajo Indian textiles and sand paintings. To the Navajo people rug-weaving is much more a passion and way of life than a craft, and the tradition of sand painting is part of their ceremony and ritual. 'I do it out of pride because my grandmother did and my mother did. I guess it is pride and tradition.' (Lenora Davis,
A Guide to Navajo Rugs, *1992)*
The Tree of Life concept has been, and still is, a very popular motif for embroiderers and stitchers from all over the world. The following design has been adapted from a Navajo rug and I have added a geometric border in bright primary colours using queen stitch, Algerian eye and cross-stitch. The two traditional figures are taken from the Mother Earth and Father Sky sand paintings.

Navajo Tree of Life

Skill Level 4
Stitch count: 136 x 183
Design size: 24.5 x 33 cm (9.75 x 13 inches)
Stitching notes: not suitable for Aida. Use two strands of stranded cotton (floss) for the cross-stitch and one strand for the back-stitch outline.

YOU WILL NEED
38 x 45 cm (15 x 18 inches) shade 16 Permin linen, 28 threads to 2.5 cm (1 inch)
Stranded cottons (floss) as listed on the chart

INSTRUCTIONS
Work a narrow hem around the edge of the linen to prevent fraying. Fold into four, press lightly and, starting to the left of a vertical thread, mark the folds with a line of tacking (basting) stitches. Start in the centre, stitch the tree, leaves and birds in cross-stitch over two threads of linen.

Add the back-stitch outline to the birds using the shade indicated on the chart.

THE DIAMOND BORDER
The diamond motifs around this design are made up of sixteen queen stitches in two-colour combinations and bordered with cross-stitch and small groups of Algerian eye stitches (see Additional stitches, page 24). The solid outline on the chart around the diamonds is not stitched but acts as a guide to your stitch position. If you are not familiar with queen stitch, try to work a few stitches on a spare piece of fabric.

If you prefer, it is possible to work the diamond shapes in cross-stitch.

When the design is complete, press lightly on the wrong side and stretch and frame as desired (see page 156).

This unusual project includes the traditional Tree of Life theme but was inspired by a Navajo woven rug. It includes a border of queen stitches and two small figures taken from sand paintings.

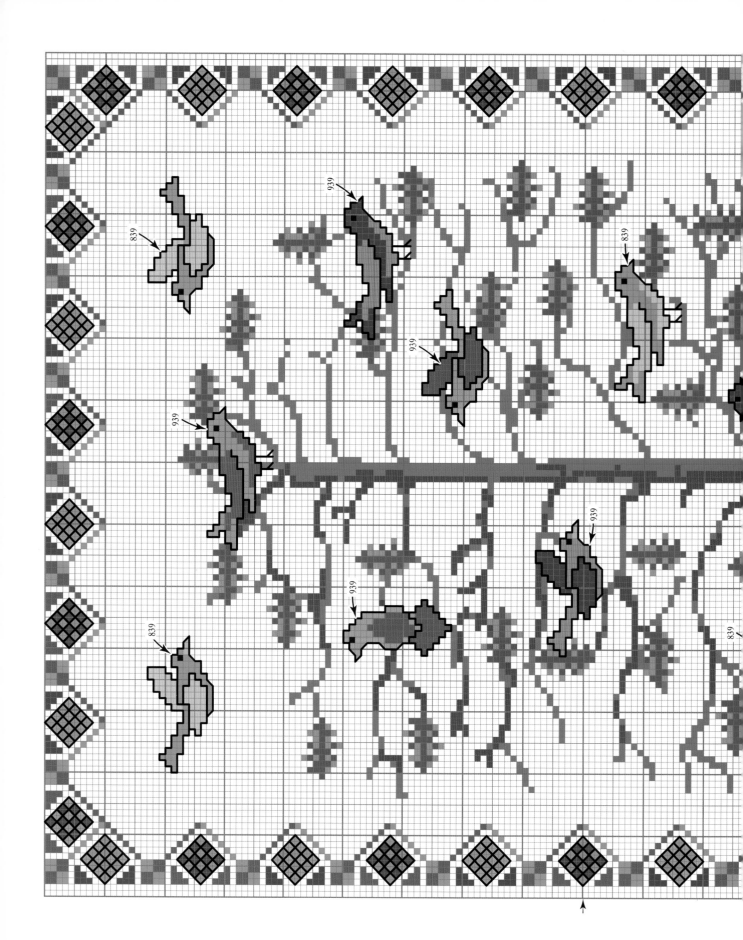

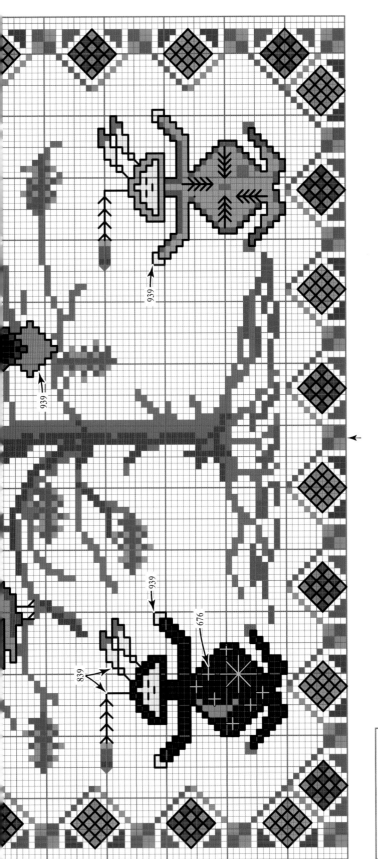

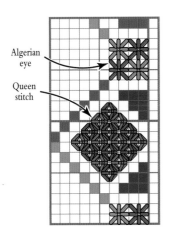

Algerian
eye

Queen
stitch

NAVAJO TREE OF LIFE
Key – DMC/Anchor

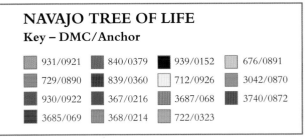

931/0921	840/0379	939/0152	676/0891
729/0890	839/0360	712/0926	3042/0870
930/0922	367/0216	3687/068	3740/0872
3685/069	368/0214	722/0323	

Birds and Bows

This romantic little project would make a lovely gift either framed as shown or mounted in a presentation card.

Skill Level 3
Stitch count: 50 x 50
Design size: 5 x 5 cm (2 x 2 inches)
Stitching notes: use one strand of stranded cotton (floss) over one thread only.

YOU WILL NEED
10 cm (4 inches) square grey linen, 25/26 threads to 2.5 cm (1 inch)
Stranded cottons (floss) of your own choice
Graph paper
Soft pencil

INSTRUCTIONS
Prepare the linen fabric as described for the Tree of Life project and set aside. Select the initials you require from the Random Letter Sampler on page 72 and copy the shapes onto your graph paper, adding the bow motif from the chart on pages 86–7. Experiment with the ribbon ends until you are satisfied with the design and then add the two birds from the Tree of Life chart.

An ideal gift for a couple: birds from the Tree of Life, simple bow motifs and initials to personalize the completed project.

Check that your design will fit your purchased frame or card (see Calculating design size, page 20).

The miniature design illustrated above is stitched using one strand of stranded cotton and is stitched over one thread only. When working the project, each cross-stitch should be worked individually rather than in two journeys.

When complete, check for missed stitches and mount or frame as preferred (see page 156).

Victorian Silk Oval

This elegant oval scene, worked on linen, was inspired by two Victorian painted and embroidered pictures from the Embroiderers' Guild Collection. The original designs were worked on silk material in a variety of stitches and were enhanced by exquisite hand painting. This delicate painting was used to add the minute detail to the faces and hands, and to add soft pastel shades to colour the background.

Victorian Ladies

Skill Level 4

Stitch count: 141 x 170
Design size: 19.5 x 24 cm (7.75 x 9.5 inches)
Stitching notes: not suitable for Aida material. Use linen or Jobelan. Use two strands of stranded cotton (floss) for the cross-stitch on the ladies and the border. Use one strand for back-stitch outline and the cross-stitched tree. Use one strand and a half cross-stitch for the grass.

YOU WILL NEED

33 x 38 cm (13 x 15 inches) cream Zweigart
  Edinburgh, 36 threads to 2.5 cm (1 inch)
Stranded cottons (floss) as listed on the chart

INSTRUCTIONS

Work a narrow hem around the edge of the linen to prevent fraying. Fold into four, press lightly and, starting to the right of a vertical thread (see Where to start, page 23), mark the folds with a line of tacking (basting) stitches.

Starting at the centre of the design and to the left of a vertical thread, begin to stitch using two strands of stranded cotton for the cross-stitch on the two figures, with the exception of the hair and faces. Remember to keep the top stitch facing the same way and finish off the loose ends as you stitch.

THE FIGURES' HAIR AND FACES

The ladies' hair is stitched in uncounted bullion and French knots (see Additional stitches, page 25) so the area to be worked will need to be outlined as follows. Thread your needle with one strand of a neutral shade of stranded cotton which will not show when the hair is complete. Looking at the chart, work a line of back-stitch outline following the route indicated by the solid line on the chart. Select wig colours (you may wish to add blonde or red shades to your palette) and begin to work the French knots inside the outlined area using two strands of stranded cotton, packing the stitches close together across the forehead and around the ears. Work the bullion knots introducing a mixture of shades (use the colour picture as your guide). Keep stitching until all the background material is well covered.

Stitch the figures' faces using one strand of stranded cotton and working over two threads of the linen. Add the backstitch to the ladies' costumes when the cross-stitch is complete.

THE TREE AND BACKGROUND SHADING

As mentioned at the beginning of this project, the Victorians loved soft pastel backgrounds to their pictures, often achieved by using watercolour paint. In this example I have softened both the foreground and the background shading as follows: work the tree trunk and leaves in complete cross-stitch but using only one strand of stranded cotton and add the foreground in half cross-stitch only.

This sumptuous oval picture is worked on linen and shows a softened foreground and background. The ladies' curly hair is achieved by working a mass of bullion knots to great effect.

I have adapted a section of the border used on Victorian Ladies for this distinctive photograph frame. The design was worked on linen using hollie point, cut and then mounted to suit this sepia-coloured picture of my family.

WILD ROSE AND HAZELNUT GARLAND

Work the border in cross-stitch using two strands of stranded cotton with the exception of the acorn cups. These may be worked in hollie point stitch (see Additional stitches, page 25) or cross-stitch (see Wild Rose Photograph Frame, page 63). Use two strands of stranded cotton for hollie point as well.

When the stitching is complete, check for any missed stitches and prepare for framing (see Finishing techniques, pages 155–6).

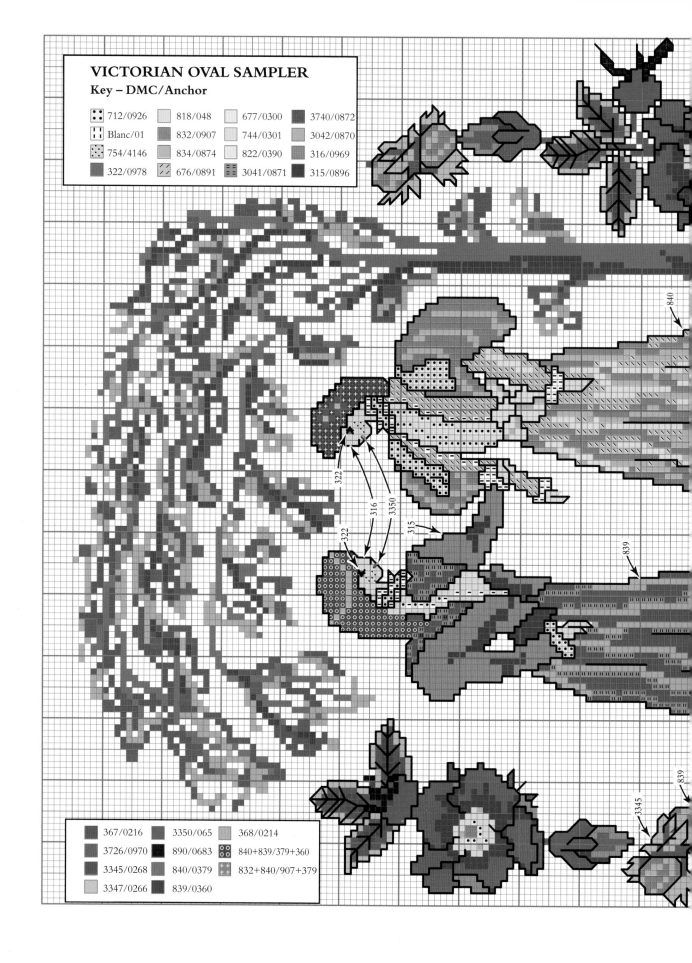

VICTORIAN OVAL SAMPLER
Key – DMC/Anchor

712/0926   818/048   677/0300   3740/0872
Blanc/01   832/0907   744/0301   3042/0870
754/4146   834/0874   822/0390   316/0969
322/0978   676/0891   3041/0871   315/0896

367/0216   3350/065   368/0214
3726/0970   890/0683   840+839/379+360
3345/0268   840/0379   832+840/907+379
3347/0266   839/0360

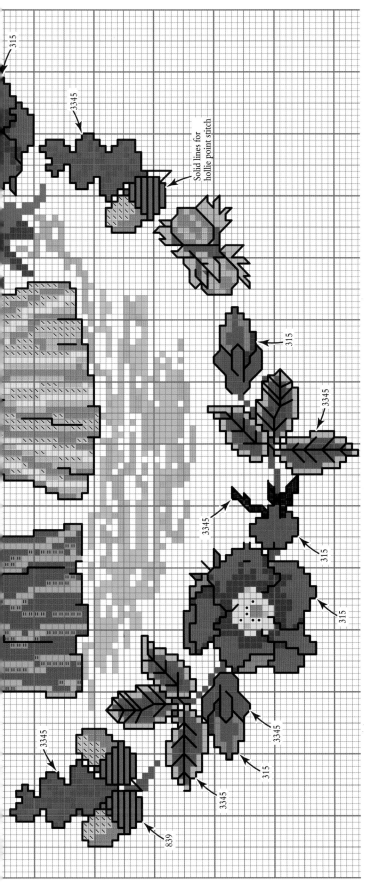

The chart contains the following labels: 315, 3345, Solid lines for hollie point stitch, 315, 3345, 3345, 315, 315, 3345, 315, 3345, 315, 3345, 839

Wild Rose Photograph Frame

This design could be used as either a mirror border or photograph frame depending on your requirements.

Skill Level 4

Stitch count: 136 x 121
Design Size: 24 x 21.5 cm (9.5 x 8.5 inches)
Stitching notes: refer to Victorian Ladies (page 59) for fabric and stitch guides.

You Will Need

37 x 34 cm (14.5 x 13.5 inches) boiled or tea-dyed linen, 30 threads to 2.5 cm (1 inch)
Stranded cottons (floss) as listed on the chart

Instructions

Prepare the fabric as for the Victorian Ladies and find the centre of your fabric. You will need to count to the border from the centre. If you find this very nerve-racking, check your design size and stitch count and measure to the approximate position. Mark with a pin and, looking at the chart, count to the edge of the fabric to double-check. When you are satisfied with the position, begin to stitch, starting from the left of a vertical thread, and complete the design as described above.

If you wish to include the hollie point stitch, proceed as follows. Select the shade required for the acorn cup and work an outline in back-stitch. Across the width of the acorn cup add the loose bars shown on the chart by a solid line and then work the detached stitch as shown in the diagram on page 25.

When the stitching is complete press lightly on wrong side and make up as described on page 154.

William Morris
Flowerpot Embroidered Cushion Cover

William Morris, who died in 1896 at the age of sixty, had tremendous influence during the Victorian era and his extraordinary legacy of designs, patterns and use of colour is very much in evidence today. During his life Morris designed ceramics, stained glass, rugs and carpets, tapestry, furniture and textiles. Many of his designs are still available in one form or another as seen in the colour picture on page 43 which features the Strawberry Thief in Liberty Lawn. The unusual colourway of this very popular design was produced to celebrate the centenary of his death.

I have based this glorious Chrysanthemum Firescreen on a simple cushion cover, probably stitched by William Morris's daughter May (1862–1938) who took over much of the designing at Morris & Co. after her father's death. The original was worked in silk and gold metallic threads and in satin stitch.

Chrysanthemum Firescreen

Skill Level 2

Stitch count: 136 x 140

Design size: 35 cm (14 inches) square

Stitching notes: suitable for Aida or linen, but remember to check that the design size is correct for your firescreen. Use three strands for the cross-stitch and two for the optional back-stitch.

YOU WILL NEED

53 cm (21 inches) square unbleached linen, 20 threads to 2.5 cm (1 inch)

Stranded cottons (floss) as listed on the chart

INSTRUCTIONS

Work a narrow hem around the edge of the linen to prevent fraying. This is important if using loose-weave linen as it frays very easily. Fold into four, press lightly and, starting to the right of a vertical thread (see How to do a cross-stitch, page 21), mark the folds with a line of tacking (basting) stitches.

Find the centre of the chart on pages 66–7 and start in the centre and to the left of a vertical thread. Begin to stitch using three strands of stranded cotton for the cross-stitch working over two threads on linen or one block if using Aida. Remember to keep the top stitch facing the same way and finish off the loose ends as you stitch by putting the needle through to the back of the work and under stitches of the same or similar colour. Snip off loose ends close to the stitching.

I have omitted the back-stitch on the example in the colour picture but if you wish to include it, refer to the suggested shade numbers on the chart. When complete, check for missed stitches, press on the wrong side (see page 148) and make up the firescreen according to the manufacturer's instructions.

This striking design is stitched on coarse unbleached linen and was adapted from a William Morris cushion cover.
This marvellous pattern would look exciting as a picture or piped cushion.

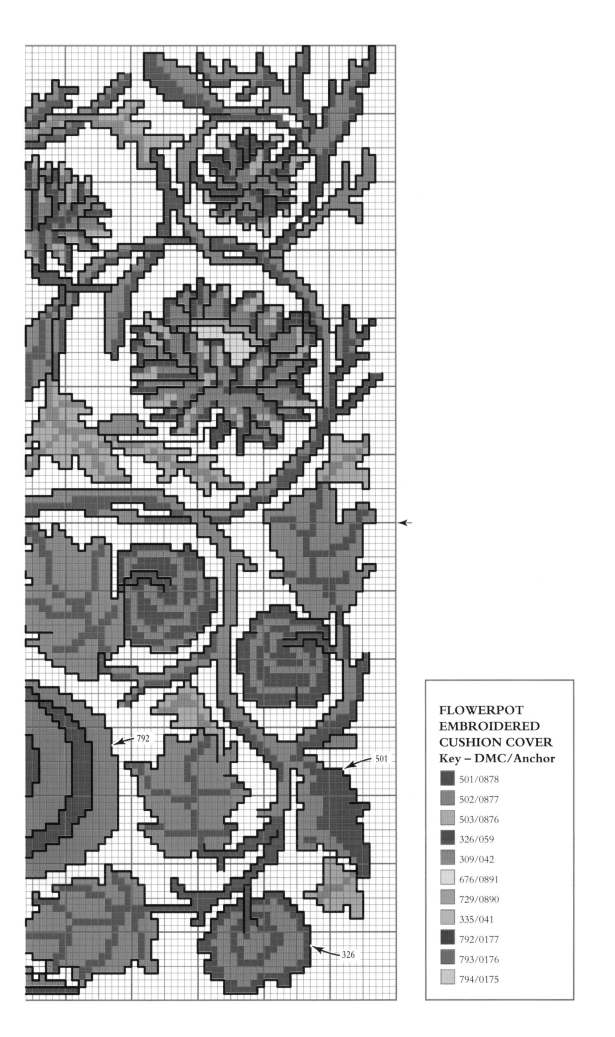

792

501

326

FLOWERPOT
EMBROIDERED
CUSHION COVER
Key – DMC/Anchor

501/0878
502/0877
503/0876
326/059
309/042
676/0891
729/0890
335/041
792/0177
793/0176
794/0175

The Lady Brabourne Sampler

This exquisite design was inspired by an embroidery seen at Parham Park in Storrington in Sussex. The original piece of work was stitched in 1917 by Lady Brabourne, although she depicted all the characters in Elizabethan costume and included motifs and flowers from that period. The stylized campaign tent above the figures in The Lovers Sampler is a familiar feature from Elizabethan and Stuart embroidery.

The Lovers Sampler

This design is worked in cross-stitch and random uncounted French knots (see page 25) and is worked on even weave. It includes a number of three-quarter cross-stitches (see page 26) with the lovers' faces being stitched over one thread to add the required detail.

Skill Level 4

Stitch count: 163 x 97
Design size: 29 x 18 cm (11.5 x 7 inches)
Stitching notes: not suitable for Aida. Use two strands of stranded cotton (floss) for the cross-stitch and one strand for the optional back-stitch outline unless stated.

YOU WILL NEED

43 x 33 cm (17 x 13 inches) 'boiled' linen,
  28 threads to 2.5 cm (1 inch)
Stranded cottons (floss) as listed on the chart
25.5 cm (10 inches) metallic gold thread

INSTRUCTIONS

Work a narrow hem around the edge of the linen to prevent fraying. Fold into four, press lightly and, starting to the right of a vertical thread (see Where to start, page 23), mark the folds with a line of tacking (basting) stitches.

Following the chart on pages 70–1 and starting in the centre to the left of a vertical thread, stitch the campaign tent, the fruit trees, the butterflies, the sun and moon as illustrated. Work over two threads of the linen in all cases.

To stitch the figures in the centre of the design as shown in the colour picture, work in cross-stitch with the exception of the faces and the wigs.

Add a few random French knots around the tree stumps and at the lovers' feet using the colours shown on the chart.

THE WIG DETAIL

The wigs are stitched in uncounted tweeded French knots (see Additional stitches, page 25) so the area to be worked will need to be outlined as follows. Thread your needle with one strand of a neutral shade of stranded cotton which will not show when the wigs are complete. Looking at the chart, work a line of back-stitch outline following the route indicated by the solid line on the chart. Select wig colours (you may wish to add blond or red shades to your palette) and begin to work the French knots inside the outlined area using one or two strands of stranded cotton and packing the stitches close together to add a curly look to the wigs. Keep stitching until all the background material is well covered.

You can experiment with the number of strands on your needle to make larger or smaller French knots and if you tweed the colours (see page 24) as you stitch, you'll achieve very interesting effects.

THE FACES

Stitch the figures' faces using one strand of stranded cotton and working over one thread of the linen following the detailed section on the chart. When the design is complete, press lightly on the wrong side and check for missed stitches. Mount and frame as desired (see page 156).

This elegant project is worked in cross-stitch and French knots and is reminiscent of early Stuart embroidery with the pretty fruit trees and charming costumes.

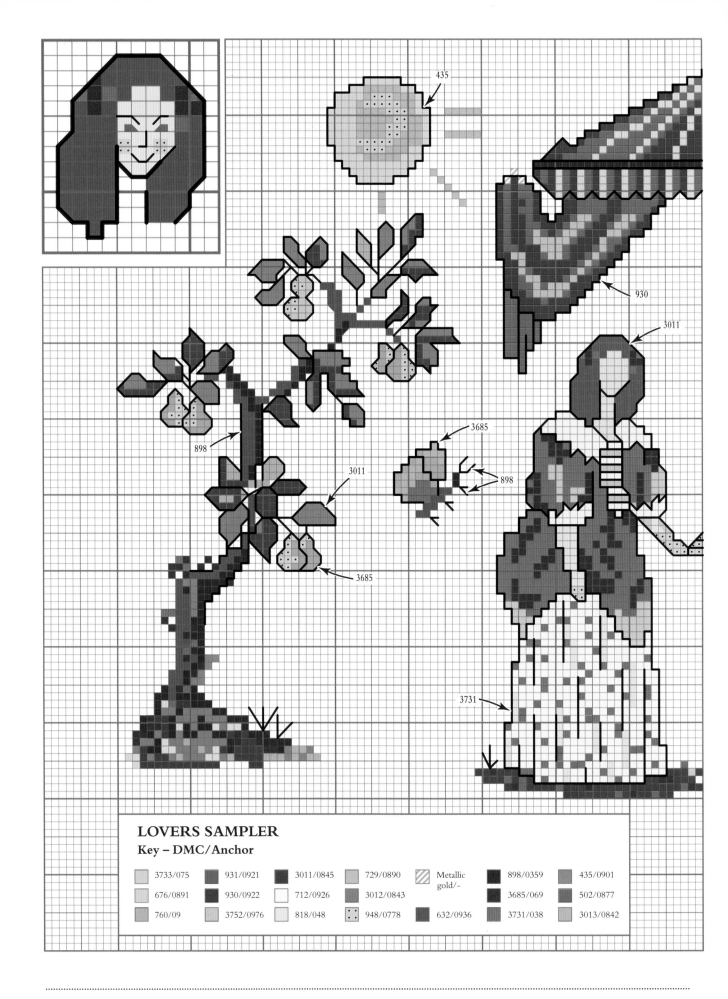

LOVERS SAMPLER
Key – DMC/Anchor

3733/075	931/0921	3011/0845	729/0890	Metallic gold/–	898/0359	435/0901
676/0891	930/0922	712/0926	3012/0843		3685/069	502/0877
760/09	3752/0976	818/048	948/0778	632/0936	3731/038	3013/0842

Alphabet Sampler

This magnificent project was inspired by two letter samplers I saw during my visit to Berlin, just months before the Wall came down. One fine example belonged to a private collector of needlework and the other, sadly, only survived as a colour illustration from the Germanisches Nationalmuseum in Nuremburg.

It seems that the tradition of young women (and a few men) spending long hours working sampler-style embroidery was almost universal in the eighteenth and nineteenth century. Working these pieces not only taught neatness and diligence but the child or young person learned the alphabet as well. In institutions it was considered an excellent way of keeping large numbers of children busy and quiet. In many cases the child would stitch moral phrases or prayers as well as adding repeated alphabets. These skills were often put to use later if the young stitcher went into service in a large household.

Random Letter Sampler

Skill Level 4

Stitch count: 286 x 251

Design size: 42 x 37 cm (16.5 x 14.5 inches)

Stitching notes: suitable for Aida or linen (see Calculating design size, page 20). Use two strands of stranded cotton (floss) for the cross-stitch over two threads of the linen and omit all the back-stitch.

YOU WILL NEED

56 x 50 cm (22 x 20 inches) unbleached linen, 36 threads to 2.5 cm (1 inch)

Stranded cottons (floss) as listed on the chart

Graph paper and soft pencil

INSTRUCTIONS

Work a narrow hem around the edge of the linen to prevent fraying. Fold into four, press lightly and, starting to the right of a vertical thread (see How to do a cross-stitch, page 21), mark the folds with a line of tacking (basting) stitches. Set aside.

Referring to the four charts on the following pages, start at the centre and to the left of a vertical thread and begin to stitch using two strands of stranded cotton for the cross-stitch. Remember to keep the top stitch facing the same way and finish off the loose ends as you stitch. Try to avoid carrying threads across unstitched areas as they will show through to the right side when the design is stretched and framed.

I have omitted the optional back-stitch outline in the example illustrated on the facing page, but you can add it in if you wish.

When the cross-stitch is complete, check for missed stitches and trim any loose ends close to the stitching. Press on wrong side as described on page 148 and mount and frame as desired (see page 156).

The largest project in the book and a spectacular one for sampler lovers. Different alphabets stitched on pure linen in bright reds and blues. Initials from this design are used throughout the book to personalize other designs.

THE ALPHABET SAMPLER

Key – DMC [Blue colourway]/Anchor

■ 321 [793]/9046	■ 350 [939]/011	□ 745 [745]/300	■ 3815 [368]/214	■ 932/343	■ 729/890
■ 349 [792]/013	□ 676 [676]/891	■ 501 [367]/878	■ 931/921	■ 3740/872	

Checked
Alphabet
Cushion
Border

939

792

Alternative colourway
for Satchel

THE ALPHABET SAMPLER
Key – DMC [Blue colourway]/Anchor

321 [793]/9046	350 [939]/011	745 [745]/300	3815 [368]/214	932/343	729/890
349 [792]/013	676 [676]/891	501 [367]/878	931/921	3740/872	

Checked Alphabet Cushion

Skill Level 2
Stitch count: 132 x 84
Design size: 24 x 15.25 cm (9.5 x 6 inches)
Stitching notes: suitable for Aida or linen, but check design size. Use two strands of stranded cotton (floss) for the back-stitch and one strand for the back-stitch outline.

You Will Need
34 x 25.5 cm (13.5 x 10 inches) ivory linen,
  28 threads to 2.5 cm (1 inch)
Stranded cottons (floss) as listed on the chart
Graph paper
Soft pencil
40 x 30 cm (16 x 12 inches) cushion pad
2 x 50 cm (20 inch) square pieces of checked linen
  fabric to make up cushion
Antique lace (see Ageing linen, page 148)

Instructions
Work a narrow hem around the edge of the linen to prevent fraying. Fold into four, press lightly and, starting to the right of a vertical thread (see How to do a cross-stitch, page 21), mark the folds with a line of tacking (basting) stitches. Set aside.

Refer to Planning layout charts on page 21 if you are unsure how to proceed. Copy the letters used for the cushion illustrated opposite or, if preferred, make your own selection. Arrange the letters in a pleasing design on the graph paper, add flower motifs and then construct the optional cross-corner frame (part of the frame is charted on page 74). When you are satisfied with the design, begin to stitch.

Start in the middle of your design and to the left of a vertical thread and cross-stitch using two strands of stranded cotton and then add any optional back-stitch. Refer to the chart for the colour suggestions.

When the cross-stitch is complete, check for missed stitches and trim any loose ends close to the stitching. Press on wrong side as described on page 148 and make up into the cushion as illustrated (refer to Finishing techniques, page 148).

Appliquéd Letter Satchel

In order to work this design on a vibrant red linen, I have changed the colourway and adapted the stranded cottons accordingly (see shades in brackets on the chart). The dimensions below will depend on the length of the name being stitched. The example in the colour illustration is made up using blue suede, but linen union would be perfectly suitable.

Skill Level 2
Stitch count: 71 x 43
Design size: 13 x 7.5 cm (5 x 3 inches)
Stitching notes: suitable for Aida or linen. Use the stranded cottons (floss) indicated in brackets on the chart, and use two strands of stranded cotton for the cross-stitch and one strand for any back-stitch outline.

You Will Need
24 x 16.5 cm (9.5 x 6.5 inches) Zwiegart red linen,
  28 threads to 2.5 cm (1 inch)
Stranded cottons (floss) as listed in brackets on the
  chart
Graph paper
Soft pencil
50 x 25.5 cm (19.75 x 10 inches) dark blue fabric or
  suede skin

Instructions
Work a narrow hem around the edge of the linen to prevent fraying. Fold into four, press lightly and, starting to the right of a vertical thread (see How to

This charming picture includes a pretty cushion trimmed with antique lace and a dark blue suede satchel incorporating the author's name. The satchel is worked on bright red linen in a blue colourway and illustrates the different effects that can be achieved.

do a cross-stitch, page 22), mark the folds with a line of tacking (basting) stitches. Set aside.

Refer to Planning layout charts on page 21 if you are unsure how to proceed. Copy the letters you require for your name or initials. Arrange the letters in a pleasing way on the graph paper, add flower motifs and, when you are satisfied with the design, calculate your fabric size (see Calculating design size, page 21). Mark the centre of your chart and begin to stitch. Remember to begin in the centre to the left of a vertical thread and keep the top stitch facing the same direction. When the cross-stitch is complete add the back-stitch (if required), check for missed stitches and make up the satchel as described on page 151.

Beaded Initial Jewel Case

The initial letter on this project has been enlarged by a simple duplication method. For each square on the chart, four stitches are formed.

Skill level 2

Stitch count: 78 x 80
Design size: 14 x 14.5 cm (5.5 x 5.75 inches)
Stitching notes: suitable for Aida and even-weave. Use two strands for the cross-stitch and one for the optional stitch outline. Add the beads using a half cross-stitch and a sharp or beading needle.

This luxurious jewel case is stitched on damask Aida and pretty detail added with coloured beads. The initial was selected from the Alphabet Sampler on page 73.

You Will Need

24 cm (9.5 inches) square cream damask Aida, 14 blocks to 2.5 cm (1 inch)
Stranded cottons (floss) as listed on the chart
1 pack each Mill Hill glass seed beads, shade numbers 02022 and 00557
Red Zweigart linen, 28 threads to 2.5 cm (1 inch)
1 size 10 sharp or beading needle
Graph paper
Soft pencil

Instructions

Work a narrow hem around the edge of the linen to prevent fraying. Fold into four, press lightly and, starting to the right of a vertical thread (see How to do a cross-stitch, page 22), mark the folds with a line of tacking (basting) stitches. Set aside.

Select the initial you wish to use on your Beaded Initial Jewel Case and copy onto your graph paper. Copy the design again, this time allowing four squares for each one on your original drawing. Add the flower motifs as preferred and when you are satisfied with the design, find and mark the centre of the chart and begin to stitch. Following your chart, work the design in cross-stitch first, add the outline in back-stitch and the beads last of all.

I have selected the beads to complement the stranded cotton and added each one on top of the cross-stitch, thus decorating two leaves and two flower centres. Select one strand in a matching shade of stranded cotton and using a half cross-stitch, add the beads, keeping each one facing the same direction.

When the design is complete, check for missed stitches and press on the wrong side (see Washing and pressing cross-stitch, page 148). Make up the Beaded Initial Jewel Case as described on page 150.

Seventeenth-century Band Sampler

The band sampler is one of the most fascinating areas of early embroidery. These long thin strips of linen were not intended to be decorative but to act as a point of reference, an aide-mémoire to the stitcher. Patterns were copied and stitched, stitches practised and when not in use the band sampler would be rolled up and put in a draw for safekeeping. The 'bands' of stitching would include cross-stitch, Algerian eye, hollie point, queen stitch and many more.
The chart on pages 86–7 is a composite of two of my favourite band samplers and has been divided into sections in the instructions. I have worked a band sampler, illustrated on page 84, excluding the Assisi section which is worked in a blue colourway below. Had I stitched the panel as part of the Band Sampler, it would have been worked in a neutral shade to imitate the original pieces.

Assisi Panel

This pretty panel is stitched in the style of Assisi work although with slight variations. Assisi embroidery uses the technique of voiding, that is, the pattern is left unstitched and the background is completely filled with cross-stitches. I have used initials from the Alphabet Sampler on page 72, so feel free to adapt these to suit.

Skill Level 1
Stitch count: 121 x 80
Design size: 21.5 x 14.5 cm (8.5 x 5.75 inches)
Stitching notes: suitable for Aida or even-weave fabric. Use two strands of stranded cotton (floss) for the cross-stitch over two threads on even-weave and one block on Aida.

You Will Need
34 x 27 cm (13.5 x 10.75 inches) Aida, 14 blocks to 2.5 cm (1 inch)
One shade of stranded cotton (floss)

A lovely, simple single-colour project which can be adapted to suit any colour scheme.

Instructions
Work a narrow hem around the edge of the Aida to prevent fraying. Fold into four, press lightly and mark the folds with a line of tacking (basting) stitches.

Following the chart on pages 86–7, start in the centre and outline the voided areas using one strand of stranded cotton. Begin the cross-stitch, filling in the background as you stitch.

When the cross-stitch pattern is complete, carefully check for missed stitches, press lightly on the wrong side (see page 148) and frame as preferred (see page 156).

Mini Bell-pull Sampler

This small project is worked on linen band and is an ideal project with which to experiment on linen. I have worked the strawberries in cross-stitch instead of queen stitch, as illustrated on the Tea-dyed Band Sampler in the colour picture on page 84. I have altered the colourway slightly and completed the bell pull with two small brass ends.

Skill Level 2

Stitch count: 112 x 39

Design size: 20 x 7 cm (8 x 2.75 inches)

Stitching notes: suitable for linen band. Use two strands of stranded cotton (floss) for the cross-stitch over two threads on even-weave.

YOU WILL NEED

35 cm (14 inches) decorated edge, half-bleached linen band – 10 cm (4 inches) wide – 28 threads to 2.5 cm (1 inch)

Stranded cottons (floss) as listed on the chart

Graph paper

Soft pencil

INSTRUCTIONS

Work a narrow hem along the raw edges of the linen band to prevent fraying. Fold into four, press lightly and, starting to the right of a vertical thread (see How to do a cross-stitch, page 22), mark the folds with a line of tacking (basting) stitches and set aside.

A small linen project stitched on linen band with Algerian eye and cross-stitch motifs.

PLANNING A LAYOUT CHART

Before begining this project, you will need to plan the position of each motif on graph paper (refer to Planning layout charts, page 21). Remember to check that your overall stitch count is within, or exactly matches, the one I have quoted.

When you are satisfied with your layout chart, start at the centre and to the left of a vertical thread and begin to stitch using two strands of stranded cotton for the cross-stitch. Remember to keep the top stitch facing the same way and finish off the loose ends as you stitch by putting the needle to the back of the work and under same or similar colours.

Snip off the loose ends close to the stitching. Try to avoid carrying threads across unstitched areas as they will show through to the right side when the design is mounted.

When the cross-stitch pattern is complete, carefully check for missed stitches, press lightly on the wrong side (see page 148), and mount as preferred (see page 156).

Tea-dyed Band Sampler

This dainty band sampler is worked on 'boiled' linen and was dipped in weak tea after the stitching had been completed. This added to the antique feel of the project. The design includes double cross-stitch, long-legged cross-stitch, four-sided stitch, queen stitch, Algerian eye, hemstitch and somersault stitch. Please refer to Additional stitches, page 23, before starting this project. If you intend to work the Assisi panel as part of your band sampler, remember to allow additional fabric.

Skill Level 5
Stitch count: 210 x 121 (excluding the Assisi panel)
Design size: 33 x 19.5 cm (13 x 7.5 inches)
Stitching notes: not suitable for Aida. Refer to the list opposite for detailed stitch instructions.

YOU WILL NEED
44.5 x 30 cm (17.5 x 12 inches) 'boiled' linen,
  32 threads to 2.5 cm (1 inch)
Stranded cottons (floss) as listed on the chart
Perle 5 in Ecru

INSTRUCTIONS
Work a narrow hem around the edge of the linen to prevent fraying. Fold into four, press lightly and, starting to the right of a vertical thread (see How to do a cross-stitch, page 21), mark the folds with a line of tacking (basting) stitches.

Starting at the centre of the design to the left of a vertical thread, begin to stitch using two strands of stranded cotton for the cross-stitch. Remember to keep the top stitch facing the same way and finish off the loose ends as you stitch.

Work each band as indicated on the chart on pages 86–7 (see page 23 for Additional stitches).

BAND	STITCHES USED
1	Double cross-stitch over four threads using two strands of stranded cotton
2a	Strawberries in queen stitch in two strands of stranded cotton over four threads
2b	Bows in cross-stitch using two strands of stranded cotton
3 and 5	Cross-stitch in two strands of stranded cotton
4	Hemstitch, drawn thread and somersault stitch in one strand of perle 5
6a	Acorns in cross-stitch with acorn cups in optional hollie point stitch
6b	Diamond eyelet (see page 85) in three strands of stranded cotton
7	Two rows double cross-stitch, each over four threads
8	Work back-stitch in one strand of stranded cotton
9	Four rows of long-legged cross-stitch in two strands of stranded cotton
10	Cross-stitch in two strands of stranded cotton
11	Four-sided stitch over four threads in two strands of stranded cotton
12	Work diamond motif in Algerian eye stitches and the small fruit tree in cross-stitch in two strands of stranded cotton
13	Double cross-stitch over four threads in two strands of stranded cotton
14	Cross-stitch in two strands of stranded cotton
15	Assisi panel (if included) in two strands of stranded cotton
16	Double cross-stitch over four threads using two strands of stranded cotton

*This band sampler has a wonderful antique feel to it, cleverly created by dipping the stitching in cold tea!
It includes double cross-stitch, long-legged cross-stitch, four-sided stitch, queen stitch, Algerian eye,
hemstitch and somersault stitch.*

The diamond eyelet motif is worked as follows: work the diamond shape in cross-stitch and then, using three strands of stranded cotton, work long stitches from each cross-stitch to the centre of the diamond. Refer to the chart for motif position.

When the design is complete, check for missed stitches and if you are intending to 'dip' your stitching, refer to Ageing linen on page 148. Press the completed project on the wrong side and frame as preferred (see page 156).

Strawberry Photograph Frame

Skill Level 1
Stitch count: 64 x 64
Design size: 12 cm (4.75 inches) square
Stitching notes: suitable for Aida or even-weave. Use two strands of stranded cotton (floss) for the cross-stitch and one for the back-stitch.

You Will Need
22 cm (8.75 inches) square Yorkshire Aida, 14 blocks to 2.5cm (1 inch)
Stranded cottons (floss) as listed on the chart
Graph paper
Soft pencil

Instructions
Work a narrow hem around the edge of the fabric to prevent fraying. Fold into four, press lightly and mark the folds with a line of tacking (basting) stitches. Set aside. (See Where to start, page 23.)

Planning A Layout Chart
Before beginning this project, you will need to plan the position of the design on graph paper (refer to Planning layout charts, page 21). It is not necessary to copy all the detail from the charts – use the outline only. The stitching can be worked from the colour charts when planned.

My children photographed in Normandy and mounted in this pretty decorated frame.

When you are satisfied with your layout chart, count from the centre point and begin to stitch using two strands of stranded cotton for the cross-stitch working over one block of Aida. If you find this very nerve-racking, check your design size, stitch-count and measure to the approximate position on the fabric. Mark with a pin and, looking at the chart, count to the edge of the fabric to double-check.

When you are satisfied with the position, begin to stitch and complete the design. Remember to keep the top stitch facing the same way and finish off the loose ends as you stitch by taking the needle to the back of the work and putting it under stitches of the same or similar colour. Snip off the loose ends close to the stitching.

When the cross-stitch is complete, add the back-stitch outline as preferred. Press lightly (see page 148) and make up as described in Finishing techniques on page 154.

SEVENTEENTH-CENTURY BAND SAMPLER
Key – DMC/Anchor

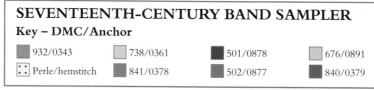

932/0343	738/0361	501/0878	676/0891
Perle/hemstitch	841/0378	502/0877	840/0379

SEVENTEENTH-CENTURY BAND SAMPLER
Key – DMC/Anchor

223/0895
224/0894
3042/0870
3041/0871
3347/0266
3348/0264
Drawn thread/perle
712/0926

Weeping Willow Sampler

*This design was inspired by the fascinating exhibition of American school samplers at the Los Angeles Country Museum of Art in 1991, and the most comprehensive study carried out by Mary Jaene Edmonds. The exhibition was so special that a book was published to complement it (*Samplers and Samplermakers: An American Schoolgirl Art 1700–1850*, published by Rizzoli International Publications Inc., 1991). I have to admit to tears when I looked at this collection of treasures. So beautiful!*

The Plantation House Sampler

Skill Level 3

Stitch count: 269 x 143

Design size: 43 x 23 cm (17 x 9 inches)

Stitching notes: suitable for Aida or even-weave fabric. Use two strands of stranded cotton (floss) for the cross-stitch over two threads on even-weave or one block on Aida.

YOU WILL NEED

56 x 35 cm (22 x 14 inches) 'boiled' or tea-dyed
  linen, 32 threads to 2.5 cm (1 inch)
Stranded cottons (floss) as listed on the chart

INSTRUCTIONS

Work a narrow hem around the edge of the linen to prevent fraying. Fold into four, press lightly and mark the folds with a line of tacking (basting) stitches. Following the chart on pages 90–1 start in the centre, beginning to the left of a vertical thread, and stitch the house, trees and border as illustrated. Work over two threads of the linen in all cases. Using one strand and a half cross-stitch, work the grass in the foreground.

Remember to keep the top stitch facing the same way and finish off the loose ends as you stitch. When the cross-stitch pattern is complete, carefully check for missed stitches, press lightly on the wrong side (see page 148), and mount and frame as preferred (see pages 155–6).

Worked on linen, this grand house sampler includes the soft blue hues and the weeping trees so often seen in American samplers of the period.

WEEPING WILLOW SAMPLER

Key – DMC/Anchor

932/0343	676/0891	501/0878	503/0876	840 + 318/0379 + 0399	301/0349
712/0926	841/0378	502/0877	840/0379	3033/0830	3766/0167

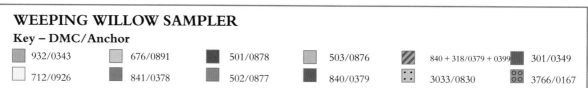

840

Work all grass in
one strand half
cross-stitch

931

501

931

WEEPING WILLOW SAMPLER
Key – DMC/Anchor

562/0210	3782/0831	807/0168	310/0403	729/0890
335/041	839/0360	806/0169	563/0208	931/0921

Embroidery From Hardanger

The designs in this section are based loosely on examples of traditional skirts and aprons from the Norsk Folkmuseum, Oslo, originally from the Hardanger region of Norway. The origins of 'Hardanger' work are not known although examples of similar work are seen in early examples of Italian needlework and Venetian lace. Norwegian drawn work (later known as Hardanger after the area of that name) thrived in that country as early as the seventeenth century and was used to decorate household linens, aprons and skirts.

Traditionally, the embroidery was worked on linen using self-coloured threads, commonly white or Ecru. The decorative elements in this type of counted needlework are the holes and cut work patterns made by the stitches. I can only give basic instructions in this section as one could devote the whole book to Hardanger but, if it inspires you, I have listed some recommended reading at the back of the book. I have added a traditional cross-stitch motif, typical of Danish samplers, as well as Norwegian star motifs and some drawn thread stitches.

Hardanger Scissor-keeper

This little scissor-weight is an ideal first Hardanger project and will teach you all the basic principles of Kloster blocks, needle weaving and dove's eyes. If you tackle this design first, none of the remaining projects in this section will present any problems.

The stitch count included below refers to the straight stitches forming the Kloster blocks.

Skill level 4
Stitch count: 30 x 30
Design size: 3 cm (1.25 inches) square
Stitching notes: this is not suitable for Aida material. You must use either even-weave or Hardanger fabric. The principle of Hardanger is that, since some threads are going to be cut and pulled out of the fabric, the stitches worked first should decorate the fabric and also prevent both damage to the remaining fabric and the disintegration of the pattern.

You Will Need
2 x 7 cm (2.75 inches) square pieces of blue Jobelan, 28 threads to 2.5 cm (1 inch)
DMC perle 5 in Ecru
DMC perle 12 in Ecru

Instructions
Work a narrow hem around the edge of one piece of fabric, keeping the other section for the back. Read through the next section referring to the diagrams before you begin to stitch.

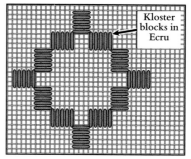

Kloster blocks

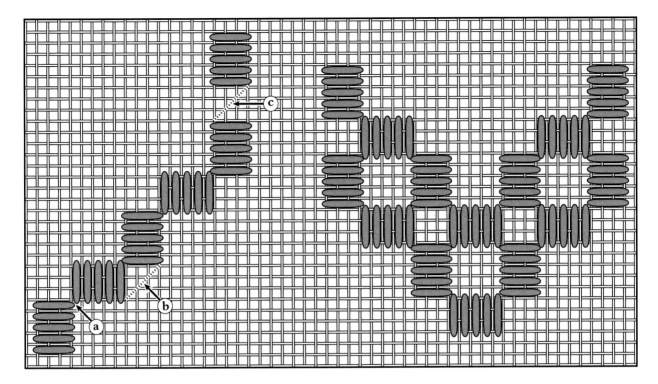

Kloster blocks
a. All corner stitches meet in the same hole.
b. Do not let thread cross over open space on the back like this.

c. When doing unconnected groups move to next group with thread at an angle on back like this.

Second row of Kloster blocks connects to the first row as above.

KLOSTER BLOCKS

These stitches form the framework for the cut areas in Hardanger and are formed by working five vertical or five horizontal straight stitches, each of them over four threads on the even-weave fabric or four blocks if working on Hardanger fabric (see diagram). The stitches are worked side by side following the threads or blocks on the fabric. They are worked in the same direction each time, and should look the same on the wrong side of the fabric.

The Kloster blocks are worked in groups or diagonal steps where the corners of the blocks share a hole (see above). They may be placed in diagonal directions but the stitches forming the blocks always follow the grain of the fabric i.e. vertical or horizontal. The blocks are worked in patterns forming enclosed areas which can then be cut and decorated.

As you work the blocks, keep checking that the stitches are counted correctly and that the blocks are opposite to each other. Look at the small chart opposite and work 12 Kloster blocks as illustrated, using one strand of perle 5 and work each straight stitch over four threads on the fabric. Work all the blocks as illustrated on the chart checking that each block has one directly opposite (as shown). Finish off any loose ends behind a block as you stitch.

CUTTING THE THREADS

This is always the area which causes anxiety and it is easy to understand why! The secret is to work all the Kloster blocks, check that you have counted correctly, and that the blocks are exactly opposite to each other.

Using very sharp, pointed scissors cut the threads at the end of the Kloster block not at the side (see diagram overleaf). The cutting side is where the

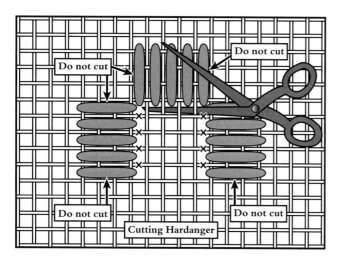

The positions marked 'x' show which threads will be cut

long straight stitches enter the fabric, not along the long edge. Take your time, cut carefully and count each thread. You will be cutting four threads at the end of each Kloster block. Pull the threads out and you should be left with something similar to the illustration below (a refers to the uncut fabric).

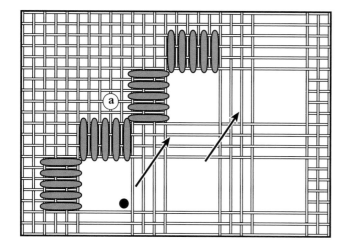

Kloster blocks cut ready for needle weaving

Needle Weaving

The threads that are left after cutting are then decorated by needle weaving (b,c and d). Looking at the diagrams opposite and using one strand of perle 12, begin to needle weave, working from right to left and taking care to keep your tension as even as possible.

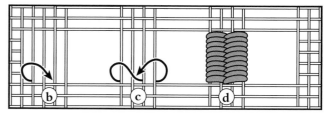

Needle weaving

Dove's Eye

This pretty decorative stitch is added while the needle weaving is worked, using one strand of perle 12 as before. Looking at the chart opposite, add the dove's eye as illustrated below.

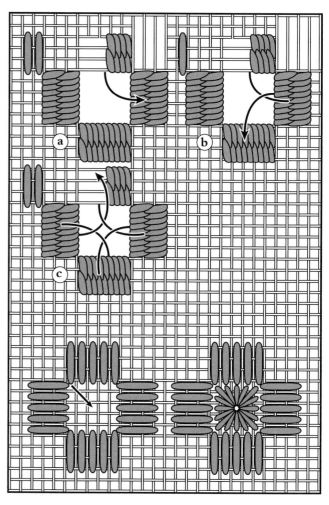

Top: dove's eye, bottom: eyelet

94

HARDANGER
Key – DMC/Anchor
■ 930/0922 ■ 931/0921

When all the stitching is complete, check that the loose ends are firmly secured and press lightly on the wrong side ready to make up as described on page 150.

Eyelet Band Pincushion

A simple project using a cross-stitch motif from the Hardanger Needlework Box and working it on eyelet linen band.

Skill level 3

Stitch count: 17 x 20
Design size: 3.75 x 3.25 cm (1.5 x 1.25 inches)
Stitching notes: not suitable for Aida material. Use an even-weave fabric. Cross-stitch is worked in two strands of stranded cotton (floss) and the back-stitch in one strand only. The Algerian eye stitches in the centre of the motif are worked in one strand of DMC perle 12 in Ecru.

YOU WILL NEED

10 cm (4 inches) eyelet linen band 7.5 cm wide
  (3 inches), 28 threads to 2.5 cm (1 inch)
Stranded cottons (floss) as listed on the chart
4 x 10 cm (4 inches) narrow blue ribbon
DMC perle 12 in Ecru
A small piece of polyester wadding

INSTRUCTIONS

Fold the eyelet band into four and mark the folds with a line of tacking (basting) stitches. Work a narrow hem along the raw edges to prevent fraying.

Work the cross-stitch from the chart on page 95, checking that the top stitches face the same direction. Add the back-stitch outline and tendrils, and the Algerian eye in one strand of perle 12 (see Additional stitches, page 24).

To make the pincushion as illustrated, fold the excess fabric to the back of the design and join the two hemmed edges with tiny running stitches. This should form a small tube with the cross-stitch motif on the front. Push a little polyester wadding into the centre of the tube and close the ends by threading lengths of ribbon through the eyelets, tying bows at the top and bottom as illustrated. An extra length of ribbon may be used to attach the pincushion to the chatelaine if desired.

Cut Work and Cross-stitch Chatelaine

I have selected the cross-stitch motif and Hardanger patterns from the Needlework Box overleaf and adapted them to fit a piece of Hardanger band. This pretty chatelaine is intended to hang around the neck with all your useful stitching aids attached to it.

The stitch count below refers to the cross-stitch motif which may be repeated as often as you wish. The design size given relates to the completed design used as the chatelaine (illustrated opposite).

Skill level 5

Stitch count: 20 x 17
Design size: 5 x 117 cm (2 x 46 inches) excluding tassels
Stitching notes: this design is not suitable for Aida material. You must use either Hardanger fabric (see the chatelaine) or an even-weave material (linen or Jobelan). The cross-stitch is worked using two strands of stranded cotton (floss) and the back-stitch is added using one strand only.

YOU WILL NEED

127 cm (50 inches) cream Hardanger band 5 cm
  wide (2 inches), 22 blocks to 2.5 cm (1 inch)
Stranded cottons (floss) as listed on the chart
DMC perle 5 in Ecru
DMC perle 12 in Ecru

The chatelaine, worked on a strip of Hardanger band, includes Kloster blocks, needle weaving and dove's eye stitches as does the scissor-keeper. The pincushion is simply worked in cross-stitch and trimmed with ribbon.

INSTRUCTIONS

Work separate narrow hems along the two raw edges of the Hardanger band to prevent it fraying. Fold the hemmed edges together and mark the central point with a short line of tacking (basting) stitches. This is the part of the chatelaine which will sit at the back of the neck. Count the blocks across the width of the band and work a line of tacking stitches down the length of the band marking the centre.

You will need to place the cross-stitch and Hardanger motifs down each side of the band, matching the positions carefully. As you will see from the photograph, I have changed the direction of the motifs so that, when worn, the designs are all the right way up. When you have planned the positions of your chosen motifs, begin to stitch, taking care to work the cross-stitch from the centre of the band.

Following the instructions for the Hardanger Scissor-keeper, work the Kloster blocks using one strand of perle 5 checking that each block has a block exactly opposite.

Cut the threads at the end of the Kloster blocks as illustrated on the chart and pull out the threads. Using one strand of perle 12, needle weave the bars and add the dove's eye stitches as preferred.

When the stitching is complete, press lightly on the wrong side and make up as follows. Measure 6 cm (2.5 inches) from the last motif on each end of the band and turn under the hemmed edge, folding to a point as illustrated in the photograph and pin into position. Carefully hem on the wrong side so that the stitching doesn't show.

MAKING TASSELS

If you wish, you may add home-made tassels to the chatelaine by proceeding as follows. Cut about twenty lengths of perle 5, roughly twice the finished length of the tassel. Tie them together in the middle using one length of perle and fold in half. Wind a long length of perle around the body of the tassel and tie off firmly. Trim the tassel to the required length and stitch to the point of the Hardanger band. Repeat for the other end of the chatelaine.

Hardanger Needlework Box

This distinctive Hardanger and cross-stitch project is carefully planned to fit the top of the luxury dark wood needlework box (see Acknowledgements, page 10). I have combined traditional drawn thread stitches as well as cross-stitch motifs to the pattern as illustrated opposite.

The stitch count below refers to the cross-stitch equivalent (see chart on page 95).

Skill Level 5

Stitch count: 86 x 118
Design Size: 24.5 x 35 cm (9.75 x 13.75 inches)
Stitching notes: not suitable for Aida material. You must use even-weave or Hardanger fabric. Remember to check your box dimension and fabric thread count and adapt if necessary. Use two strands for the cross-stitch and two strands for the back-stitch detail. One strand of perle 5 should be used for the Algerian eye stitches.

YOU WILL NEED
56 x 43 cm (22 x 17 inches) Floba (linen-style fabric), 18 threads to 2.5 cm (1 inch)
DMC perle 5 in Ecru
DMC perle 12 in Ecru
Stranded cottons (floss) as listed on the chart
Contrasting fabric to mount behind the completed project (I used dark blue damask to co-ordinate with our furnishings)

INSTRUCTIONS
Work a narrow hem around the edge of the linen to prevent fraying. Fold into four, press lightly and, starting to the left of a vertical thread, mark the folds with a line of tacking (basting) stitches.

Following the chart on page 95 start in the centre and work the Kloster blocks using one strand of perle 5. Remember that each block is made up of five straight stitches, all of which are worked over four threads. As you stitch keep checking that every Kloster block has a similar block directly opposite. When all the Kloster blocks are complete, check for any loose ends and any miscounts!

Work the cross-stitch motif in the centre of the diamond shapes as shown on the chart, adding the Algerian eye in one strand of perle 5. Add the back-stitch using two strands of stranded cotton. Work the star shapes in satin stitch (see Additional Stitches, page 26) using one strand of perle 5.

Cutting the Threads

When all the cross-stitch and satin stitches are complete, cut the threads at the end of the Kloster blocks as shown on the chart. Use a small pair of sharp, pointed scissors and cut one section at a time. Looking at the chart, needle weave the bars as illustrated, adding dove's eye stitches as preferred.

Only the four central threads are removed in each direction for the last two diamond sections (see cutting guide on the chart). Using one strand of perle 5, work somersault stitches along the drawn threads (see Additional Stitches, page 24).

When all the stitching is complete, check carefully for loose ends or threads, press lightly on the wrong side and make up the box according to the manufacturer's instructions.

....

The cover for this wooden needlework box is worked on Floba fabric and includes Kloster blocks, needle weaving, dove's eye, cross-stitch and somersault stitch. The stitching is mounted on blue fabric to co-ordinate with our furnishings.

Stumpwork Mirror

This exquisite design was inspired by the stumpwork mirror in the library at Sudeley Castle, Gloucestershire. The original, much larger design was set in a bamboo frame made of many sections dividing the wonderful three-dimensional needlework into simple stories.

Stuart Mirror

Skill Level 4

Stitch count: 112 x 152

Design size: 20 x 27.5 cm (8 x 11 inches)

Stitching notes: suitable for Aida or linen. Use two strands of stranded cotton (floss) for the cross-stitch over two threads of the linen. The grass and the water in the fountain are stitched in half cross-stitch using one strand of stranded cotton. Add the back-stitch detail in one strand only. The figures' heads and faces are stitched using the same technique as the Victorian Ladies (see page 59).

YOU WILL NEED

33 x 40 cm (13 x 16 inches) Jobelan shade 157, 28 threads to 2.5 cm (1 inch)

Stranded cottons (floss) as listed on the chart

12 small gold sequins

INSTRUCTIONS

Work a narrow hem around the edge of the linen to prevent fraying. Fold into four, press lightly and, starting to the right of a vertical thread (see How to do a cross-stitch, page 21), mark the folds with a line of tacking (basting) stitches.

Count from the centre tacking to the beginning of the stitching and, starting to the left of a vertical thread, begin to stitch using two strands of stranded cotton for the cross-stitch. Remember to keep the top stitch facing the same way and finish off the loose ends as you stitch. Try to avoid carrying threads across unstitched areas as they will show through to the right side when the design is stretched and framed.

THE WIGS AND FACES

The wigs are stitched in uncounted tweeded French knots (see Additional stitches, page 25) so the area to be worked will need to be outlined as follows. Thread your needle with one strand of a neutral shade of stranded cotton which will not show when the wigs are complete. Looking at the chart, work a back-stitch outline following the route indicated by the solid line. Select wig colours and begin to work the French knots inside the outlined area using one or two strands of stranded cotton, packing the stitches close together to add a curly look to the wigs. Keep stitching until all the background material is well covered.

Stitch the figures' faces using one strand of stranded cotton and work over one thread of the linen following the detailed section on the chart.

This stunning project was inspired by the stumpwork mirror in the library at Sudeley Castle and is a personal favourite of mine! The design is stitched on Jobelan and I have added small gold sequins at random and a mirror tile to finish.

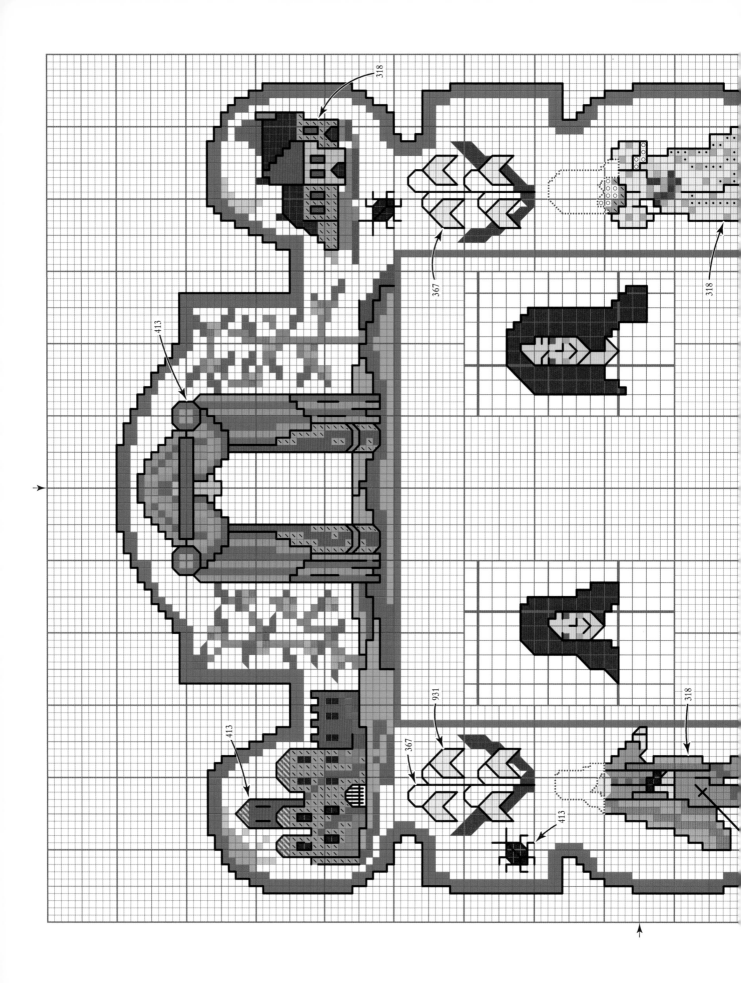

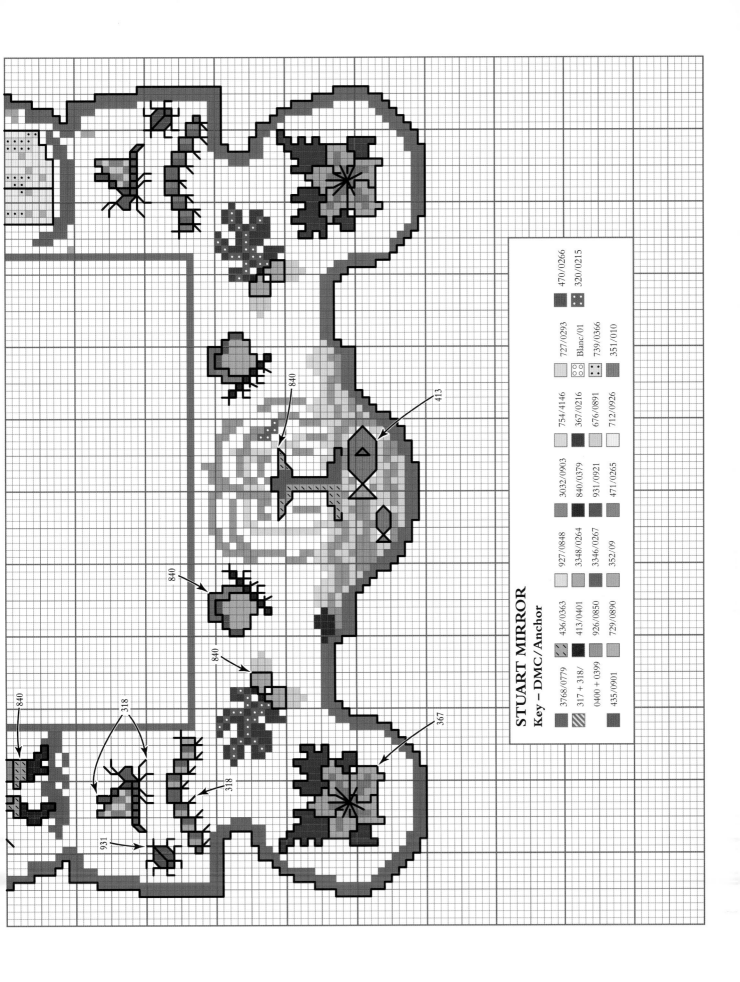

STUART MIRROR
Key – DMC / Anchor

3768/0779	436/0363	927/0848
317 + 318/	413/0401	3348/0264
0400 + 0399	926/0850	3346/0267
435/0901	729/0890	352/09

3032/0903	754/4146	727/0293
840/0379	367/0216	Blanc/01
931/0921	676/0891	739/0366
471/0265	712/0926	351/010

470/0266	
320/0215	

When the cross-stitch is complete, check for missed stitches and trim any loose ends close to the stitching. Add the optional sequins and beads at random using a half cross-stitch and one strand of a neutral shade of stranded cotton. Press on wrong side as described on page 148 and mount as described on page 154.

Flower Key-keeper

This dainty project is an ideal gift and may be stitched in an evening. The little padded cushion is joined together using long-legged cross-stitch in matching stranded cotton.

Skill Level 2
Stitch count: 20 x 22
Design size: 5 x 5.5 cm (2 x 2.25 inches)
Stitching notes: suitable for Aida or even-weave fabric. Use three strands of stranded cotton (floss) for the back-stitch and one strand for the back-stitch outline.

YOU WILL NEED
10 cm (4 inches) square unbleached linen, 20
 threads to 2.5 cm (1 inch)
Stranded cottons (floss) as listed on the chart
20 Mill Hill glass seed beads, shade number 00020
Beading or sharp needle
Gold-coloured miniature key or charm

INSTRUCTIONS
Work a narrow hem round the edge of the linen to prevent fraying. Fold into four, press lightly and, starting to the right of a vertical thread (see Where to start, page 23), mark the folds with a line of tacking (basting) stitches.

Starting in the middle of your design and to the left of a vertical thread, use three strands of stranded cotton for the cross-stitch and then add any optional

back-stitch, referring to the chart for suggested colours. To finish off stitches, take the needle to the back and under stitches of the same or similar colour. Snip off loose ends close to the stitching.

When the cross-stitch is complete, check for missed stitches and trim any loose ends close to the stitching. Add the optional beads on top of the cross-stitch using one strand of stranded cotton and a half cross-stitch. Add the charm if desired, press on wrong side as described on page 148 and make into a key-keeper (refer to Finishing techniques on page 150) as illustrated.

Embroidered Shaker Box

I have selected motifs from the charts on pages 102–3 to decorate this beautiful Shaker box. As with any made-to-measure project, it is easier to select the box or frame before you start so that you can adapt the design to suit. A stitched box like this would make a lovely wedding gift, so why not match the hair colour to that of the bride and groom? Try changing the hair colours using mixtures of light and dark shades.

Skill Level 3
Stitch count: 101 x 46
Design size: 15 x 7.5 cm (6 x 3 inches)
Stitching notes: suitable for Aida or linen. Use two strands of stranded cotton (floss) for the cross-stitch and one strand for any back-stitch outline.

YOU WILL NEED
28 x 16.5 cm (11 x 6.5 inches) parchment Jobelan,
 32 threads to 2.5 cm (1 inch)
Stranded cottons (floss) as listed on the chart

INSTRUCTIONS
Work a narrow hem around the edge of the linen to prevent fraying. Fold into four, press lightly and,

This lovely hand-made box has been decorated with motifs from the Stuart Mirror, adding a simple twisted cord edging.

starting to the right of a vertical thread (see How to do a cross-stitch, page 22), mark the folds with a line of tacking (basting) stitches.

Work the two figures, with the exception of their faces and hair, from the chart adding the insects and flowers as preferred. Next, add the faces as described on page 100, adding the French knot wigs when the faces are complete.

When the cross-stitch is complete, check for any missed stitches and make up as instructed by the manufacturer.

Lily of the Valley Bookmark

Skill Level 2

Stitch count: 41 x 14

Design size: 19 x 2.5 cm (7.5 x 1 inch) complete bookmark measurement

Stitching notes: not suitable for Aida fabric because of the three-quarter stitches. Use two strands of stranded cotton (floss) for the cross-stitch and one for any back-stitch outline.

YOU WILL NEED

28 cm (11 inches) half-bleached eyelet band 5 cm wide (2 inches), 28 threads to 2.5 cm (1 inch)

Stranded cottons (floss) as listed on the chart

50 cm (19.75 inches) very narrow bright blue ribbon

1 pack each Mill Hill glass pebble beads in shades 05168, 05147 and 05021

INSTRUCTIONS

Work a narrow hem along the raw edges of the eyelet band. Fold in half lengthways and mark the fold with a line of tacking (basting) stitches. Looking at the chart, work the lily motifs in blue and white as illustrated. Add the back-stitch detail and finish off any loose ends by putting the needle to the back of the work and under stitches of the same or similar colour. Snip off the loose ends close to the stitching.

Press the bookmark lightly on the wrong side and complete as follows. Thread the narrow ribbon through the eyelets and anchor at the top of the bookmark by working a row of tiny back stitches across the width of the band. This line of stitches allows the top edge of the bookmark to be frayed successfully. Turn the ribbon at the top edge and weave back down the eyelets again, this time from the wrong side.

Fold the bottom of the bookmark to a point as illustrated, bringing the four ribbon ends out

Worked on a piece of eyelet linen band and threaded with narrow ribbon, this pretty bookmark would make a lovely gift. The flower motifs are taken from the Stuart Mirror design illustrated on page 101.

through the point. Thread these loose ends with the beads as illustrated in the colour picture.

Stitching Paper Flower Bookmark

You will need to select the motifs you wish to use on your bookmark from the chart for the Stuart Mirror. The stitch count below refers to the example in the colour picture and includes the cutting line on the parchment stitching paper. Refer to page 18 for the stitching techniques used on stitching paper.

Skill Level 2
Stitch count: 23 x 92
Design size: 4.5 x 17.75 cm (1.75 x 7 inches)
Stitching notes: not suitable for Aida or even-weave fabric. The design is stitched on stitching paper. Use three strands of stranded cotton (floss) for the cross-stitch and two strands for any back-stitch outline.

You Will Need

3 sheets 25 x 7.5 cm (10 x 3 inches) each stitching paper in parchment, holly green and gold, 14 blocks to 2.5 cm (1 inch)
Stranded cottons (floss) as listed on the chart
Narrow ribbon or ribbon floss in co-ordinating colours to trim the bookmark (optional)

Instructions

Select the motifs you wish to include on the bookmark and, looking at the chart, work the cross-stitch and add the back-stitch outline as necessary.

When the stitching is complete, check for missed stitches and complete as follows. Using a sharp pair of scissors or a craft knife cut a simple decorative edge around the stitching. You may find it useful to draw the edge on the wrong side with a soft pencil. Cut the remaining sheets of stitching paper, also with a decorative edge, but a little larger each time. Using a little double-sided adhesive tape, stick the three sections together and trim with matching ribbons.

Using designs from the Stuart Mirror, this bookmark is stitched on stitching paper, cut to size and trimmed with ribbons.

Victorian Crazy Patchwork

*This wonderful, wild, colourful design was inspired by a piece of patchwork seen at
The Art Institute, Chicago, and was developed by finding an exquisite piece of crazy patchwork in
an antique shop in Scotland.*

Crazy Patchwork Sampler

Skill Level 3
Stitch count: 226 x 125
Design size: 40.5 x 23 cm (16 x 9 inches)
Stitching notes: suitable for Aida or even-weave
fabric. Use two strands of stranded cotton (floss) for
the cross-stitch over two threads on even-weave or
one block if Aida fabric. The decorative stitches as
shown in the photograph opposite are added at random when the cross-stitch is complete.

YOU WILL NEED
56 x 35.5 cm (22 x 14 inches) ivory linen, 28 threads
  to 2.5 cm (1 inch)
Stranded cottons (floss) as listed on the chart
Assorted beads, sequins and charms
Various coloured threads for surface embroidery

INSTRUCTIONS
Work a narrow hem around the edge of the linen to
prevent fraying. Fold into four, press lightly and
mark the folds with a line of tacking (basting)
stitches. Following the charts on pages 110–11 and

starting in the centre, begin to the left of a vertical
thread and work the cross-stitch. Complete each
coloured section before moving on to a new colour.

When the cross-stitch pattern is complete, carefully check for missed stitches and then you can go a
little wild! Select contrasting-coloured stranded
cottons, rayon threads and metallics and work lines
of herringbone at random (see Additional stitches,
page 25).

ADDING TRIMMINGS
Lay the completed project face up on a clean flat
surface and experiment with your trimmings until
you are satisfied with the design. Try grouping
beads and sequins together, making tassels with
sparkly threads, dangling crystal beads or even attaching feathers.

When the design is complete, check for missed
stitches and mount and frame as desired (see pages
155–6).

*This extravagant folly is wonderful to stitch! There are no rules, so you can
wax as lyrical as you like.*

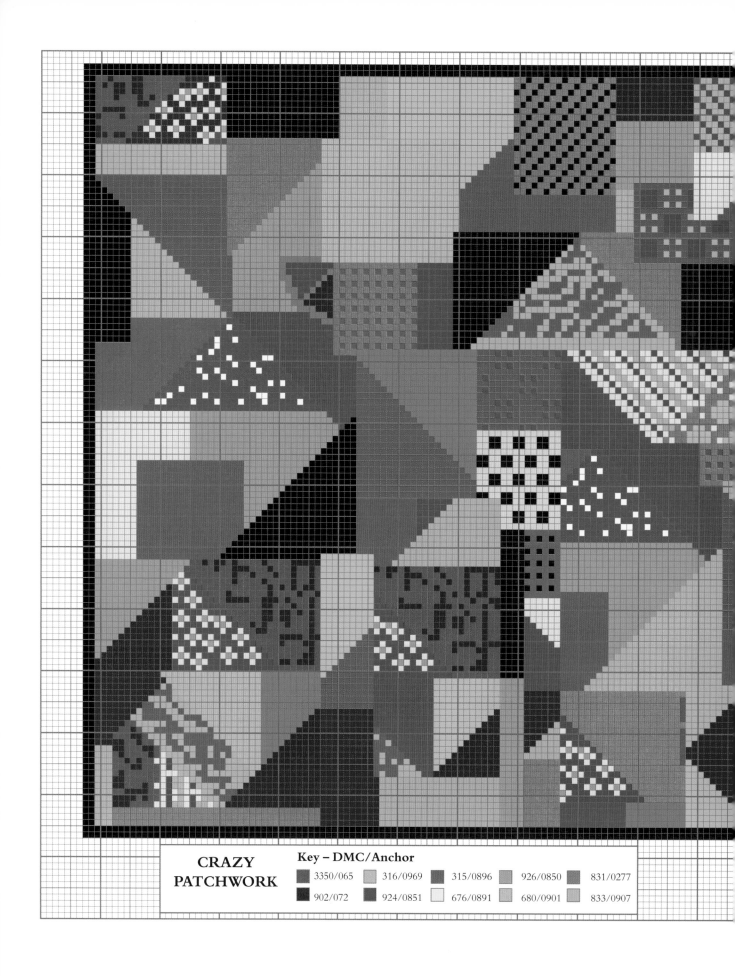

CRAZY
PATCHWORK

Key – DMC/Anchor

3350/065	316/0969	315/0896	926/0850	831/0277
902/072	924/0851	676/0891	680/0901	833/0907

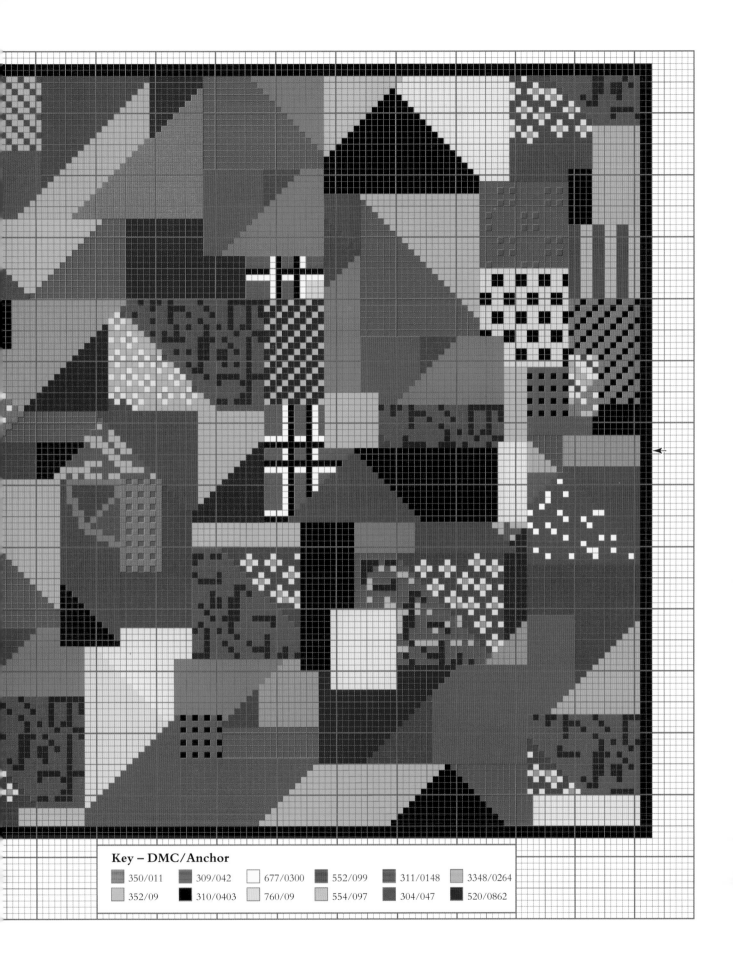

Key – DMC/Anchor

350/011	309/042	677/0300	552/099	311/0148	3348/0264
352/09	310/0403	760/09	554/097	304/047	520/0862

Beaded Treasure Album

Skill Level 2
Stitch count: 164 x 77
Design size: 30 x 14 cm (11.75 x 5.5 inches)
Stitching notes: suitable for Aida or even-weave fabric. I have exchanged DMC 316 for a shiny perle 3350 to add lustre. Use two strands of stranded

This little treasure album, made to keep those special mementos, a lock of hair or a faded photograph, is a simple version of the Crazy Patchwork Sampler.

*A treasure album to keep those special memories – a lock of hair, a poem, a photograph,
anything you wish to keep safe – and a spectacles case to wear around your neck, both stitched using sections of the
Crazy Patchwork Sampler on page 109. Use beads, sequins, stars and rhinestones to add a sparkle!*

cotton (floss) for the cross-stitch, or one strand of perle over two threads on even-weave or one block if using Aida fabric.

YOU WILL NEED
43 x 24 cm (17 x 9.5 inches) cream Aida, 14 blocks to 2.5 cm (1 inch)
Stranded cottons (floss) as listed on the chart
Assorted beads, sequins and charms
1 skein perle 3350

INSTRUCTIONS
Work a narrow hem around the edge of the Aida to prevent fraying. Fold into four, press lightly and mark the folds with a line of tacking (basting) stitches. Select the section(s) of the pattern to be stitched and carefully cover the remaining chart with removable sticky paper. The project may be stitched from the book without the need to redraw.

Start in the centre of the visible pattern, work the cross-stitch and complete each coloured section before moving on to a new colour.

When the cross-stitch is complete, add the trimmings as described for the Crazy Patchwork Sampler. Make up into the Treasure Album as described in the Making books section on page 153.

Crazy Panel Spectacle Case

As with the Treasure Album this useful, colourful spectacle case is stitched using a section of the chart for the Crazy Patchwork Sampler. The stitched panel is inset into a piece of black velvet.

Skill Level 2
Stitch count: 77 x 35
Design size: 14 x 6.25 cm (5.5 x 2.5 inches)
Stitching notes: suitable for Aida or even-weave fabric. Use two strands of stranded cotton (floss) for the cross-stitch over two threads on even-weave or one block if using Aida fabric.

YOU WILL NEED
24 x 16.5 cm (9.5 x 6.5 inches) cream Aida, 14 blocks to 2.5 cm (1 inch)
Stranded cottons (floss) as listed on the chart
45.5 x 13 cm (18 x 5 inches) black velvet and 1.25 metres (49 inches) of satin binding
Black sequins (optional)

INSTRUCTIONS
Work a narrow hem around the edge of the Aida to prevent fraying. Fold into four, press lightly and mark the folds with a line of tacking (basting) stitches. Select and work the crazy patchwork as described above, starting in the centre of the visible pattern and working the cross-stitch over one block of the Aida fabric.

When the cross-stitch is complete, add the optional black sequins at random as described for the Crazy Patchwork Sampler. Press lightly on the wrong side (see page 148) and make up as described on page 151.

Hand-painted Berlin Chart

This glorious colourful pattern has been adapted from my small but precious collection of Victorian Berlin charts. Berlin wool was introduced from the German city of that name in the early 1800s, and with the wool came the wonderful hand-painted needlework patterns. There had been needlework charts for many years but the first documented coloured chart appeared in 1804.
These hand-painted charts were interpreted using wool, silk and beads and were worked on linen, gauze and canvas.

Victorian Rose Footstool

This sumptuous footstool pattern is worked in stranded cottons on linen – and should be used for decorative purposes only! If you would like to be able to put your feet on the footstool, I have included an alternative colour key for Appleton crewel wool to be used on suitable canvas. Remember to re-calculate the design size of the finished piece if you are altering the materials. The design size quoted below relates to the footstool I have selected, not the size of the stitched area.

Skill Level 2
Stitch count: 127 x 133
Design size: 40.5 cm (16 inches) in diameter
Stitching notes: suitable for canvas or even-weave fabric. Use two strands of stranded cotton (floss) for the cross-stitch, over two threads on even-weave.

You Will Need
50 cm (19.75 inches) square Wichelt Heatherfield, 28 threads to 2.5 cm (1 inch)
Stranded cottons (floss) as listed on the chart

APPLETON EXCHANGE LIST

DMC	APPLETON	DMC	APPLETON
326	948	309	946
335	945	899	944
729	695	676	472
745	471	319	406
367	403	320	401
368	421	632	305

Instructions
Work a narrow hem around the edge of the linen to prevent fraying. Fold into four, press lightly and, starting from the right of a vertical thread (see How to do a cross-stitch, page 21), mark the folds with a line of tacking (basting) stitches.

Follow the chart on pages 116–17 and start at the centre, beginning to the left of a vertical thread. Work the cross-stitch and check your position as you stitch.

When the cross-stitch pattern is complete, carefully check for missed stitches, press lightly on the wrong side (see page 148) and make up the footstool as described on page 154.

Adapted from my own Berlin charts, this footstool looks and feels Victorian!
Worked in cross-stitch on linen, it has a fine delicate quality. It could be stitched using wool and canvas
to make a more hard-wearing piece of furniture.

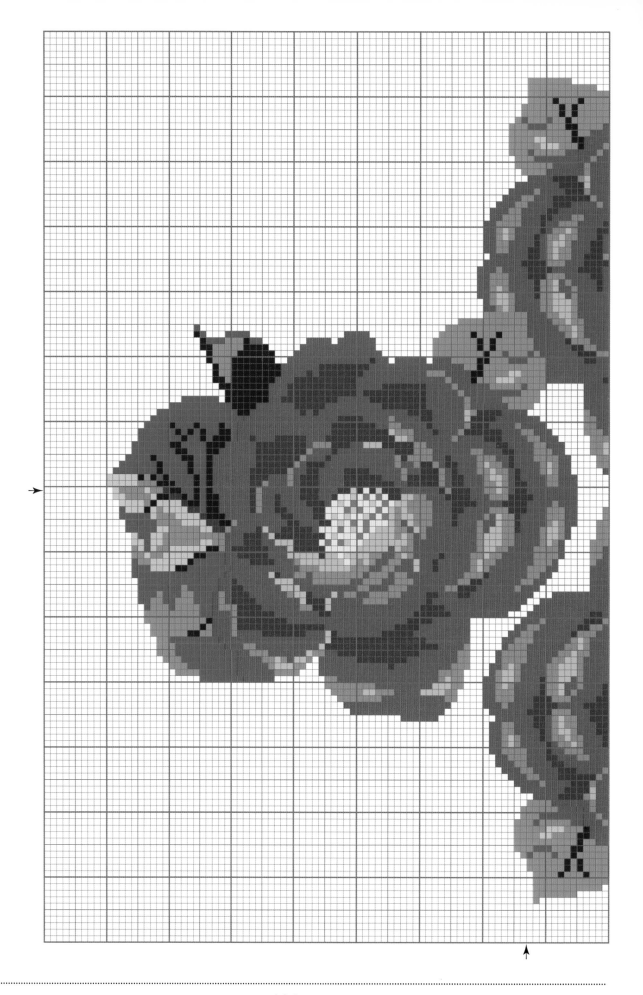

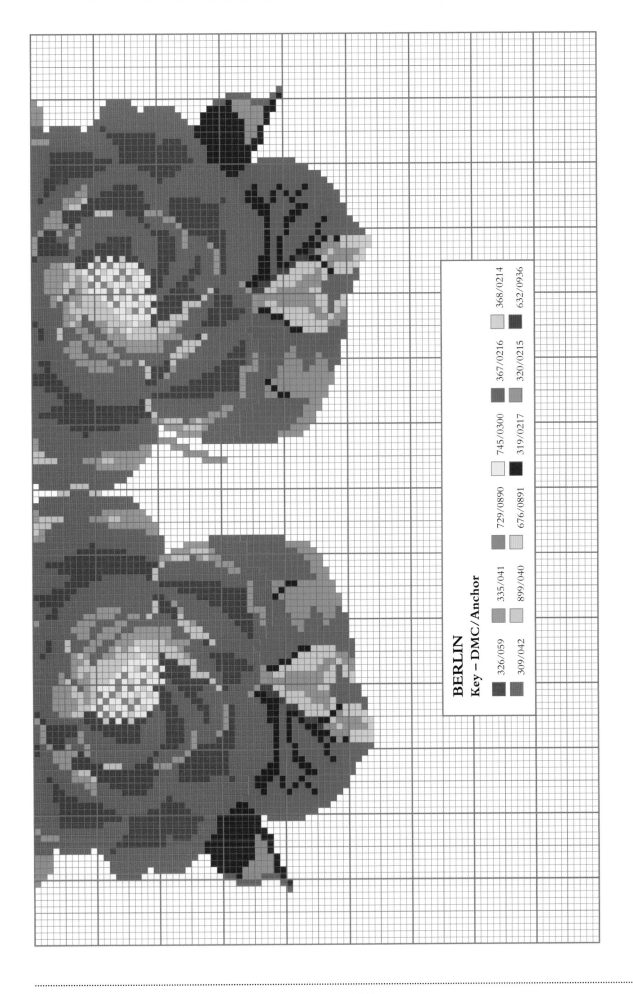

BERLIN
Key – DMC / Anchor

326/059
309/042
335/041
899/040
729/0890
676/0891
745/0300
319/0217
367/0216
320/0215
368/0214
632/0936

The Sheldon Tapestries

I visited Hatfield House as part of a stitching weekend and was fortunate enough to tour the Textile Conservation area. This stately home houses The Four Seasons, some of the most exciting Sheldon Tapestries, and I was fascinated to observe the careful repair of Winter during my visit. Another famous Sheldon Tapestry occupies the main wall in the library at Sudeley Castle in Gloucestershire. I love these tapestries! Every time I look at the exquisite craftsmanship, all completed in the late sixteenth century, I find more to admire.

I have chosen small flower and insect motifs for this project, although I could have devoted the whole book to needlework inspired by these works of art.

Oak Leaf and Acorn Candlescreen

This idea is a replica of the little candlescreen used in the days before electricity and makes an unusual ornament. The oak leaf and acorn would make an ideal motif for a stitched card or wooden box.

Skill Level 1
Stitch count: 39 x 48
Design size: 7.5 x 9 cm (3 x 3.5 inches)
Stitching notes: suitable for even-weave and Aida. Use two strands of stranded cotton (floss) for the cross-stitch and one strand for the back-stitch.

You Will Need
15 x 20 cm (6 x 8 inches) rustico Aida, 14 blocks to 2.5 cm (1 inch)
Stranded cottons (floss) as listed on the chart

Stitched on rustico Aida, this simple cross-stitch project has an added dimension in this pretty reproduction candlescreen.

This enchanting flower sampler, based on the flower styles of Sheldon Tapestry, is worked on green Jobelan and includes some of the pretty little insects found on needlework of this period. The dragonfly's wings are stitched using blending filament to add the gossamer sparkle.

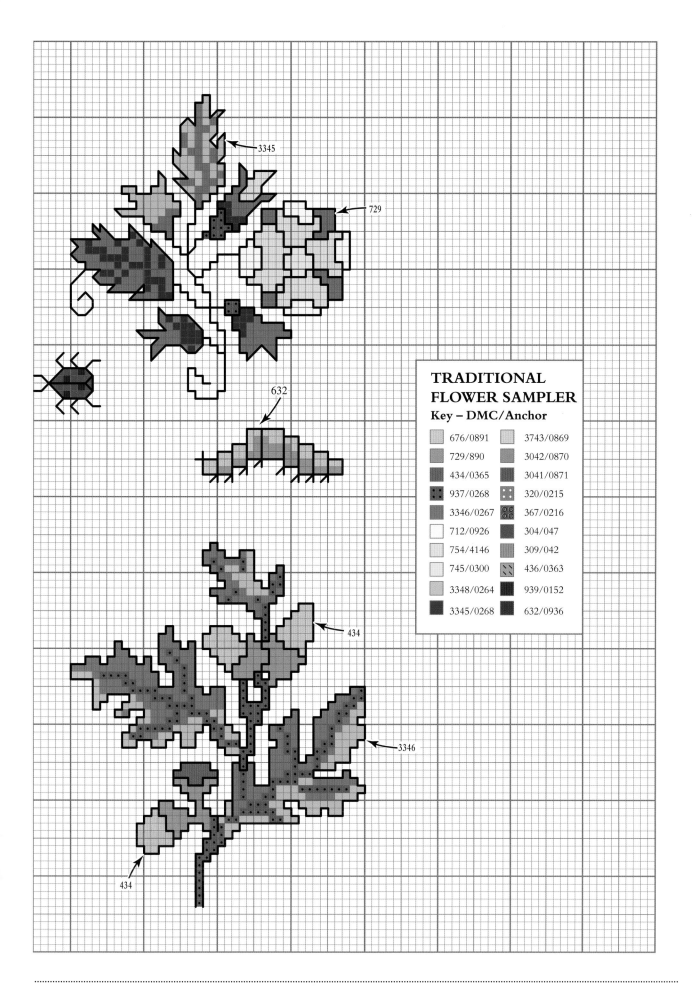

TRADITIONAL
FLOWER SAMPLER
Key – DMC/Anchor

676/0891		3743/0869	
729/890		3042/0870	
434/0365		3041/0871	
937/0268		320/0215	
3346/0267		367/0216	
712/0926		304/047	
754/4146		309/042	
745/0300		436/0363	
3348/0264		939/0152	
3345/0268		632/0936	

INSTRUCTIONS

Work a narrow hem around the edge of the Aida to prevent fraying. Fold into four, press lightly and mark the folds with a line of tacking (basting) stitches.

Looking at the chart on pages 120–1, find the centre of the acorn motif and, starting at the centre of the design, begin to stitch using two strands of stranded cotton for the cross-stitch. Remember to keep the top stitch facing the same way and finish off the loose ends as you stitch by putting the needle to the back of the work and under stitches of the same or similar colour. Snip off the loose ends close to the stitching.

Add the optional back-stitch when the cross-stitch is complete, press on the wrong side (see page 148) and make up according to manufacturer's instructions.

Traditional Flower Sampler

This simple but elegant project is stitched on green Jobelan fabric but would look equally dramatic on black or navy blue. To add the shine to the dragonfly's wings I have combined a blending filament with the stranded cotton. You might try adding beads to the strawberries or gold threads to the insects.

Skill Level 2
Stitch count: 120 x 107
Design size: 23 x 19 cm (9 x 7.5 inches)
Stitching notes: suitable for Aida and even-weave.

Use two strands of stranded cotton (floss) for the cross-stitch and one strand for the back-stitch.

YOU WILL NEED
43 x 38 cm (17 x 15 inches) charcoal green Jobelan, 28 threads to 2.5 cm (1 inch)
Stranded cottons (floss) as listed on the chart
Balger blending filament in confetti shades

INSTRUCTIONS

Work a narrow hem around the edge of the fabric to prevent fraying. Fold into four, press lightly and, starting to the right of a vertical thread (see How to do a cross-stitch, page 21), mark the folds with a line of tacking (basting) stitches.

Starting at the centre of the fabric and to the left of a vertical thread, begin to stitch using two strands of stranded cotton for the cross-stitch. Remember to keep the top stitch facing the same way. There are a number of three-quarter stitches included in this design, so refer to Additional stitches on page 26 if you have not worked these before. Finish off the loose ends as you stitch by putting the needle to the back of the work and under stitches of the same or similar colour. Snip off the loose ends close to the stitching.

To stitch the dragonfly's wings, combine one strand of Balger blending filament with two strands of stranded cotton. If you find the blending filaments tangle a little, use slightly shorter lengths of threads in your needle.

When the stitching is complete, press lightly on the wrong side (see page 148) and frame as preferred (see page 156).

French Crewel Panel

This extraordinary bird design was taken from the wonderful French crewel pattern (shown in the colour picture below) which was originally part of a double-bed cover made up of six decorative panels. The original design would have been drawn or traced onto the fabric and then stitched using buttonhole, satin, chain and split stem stitch.

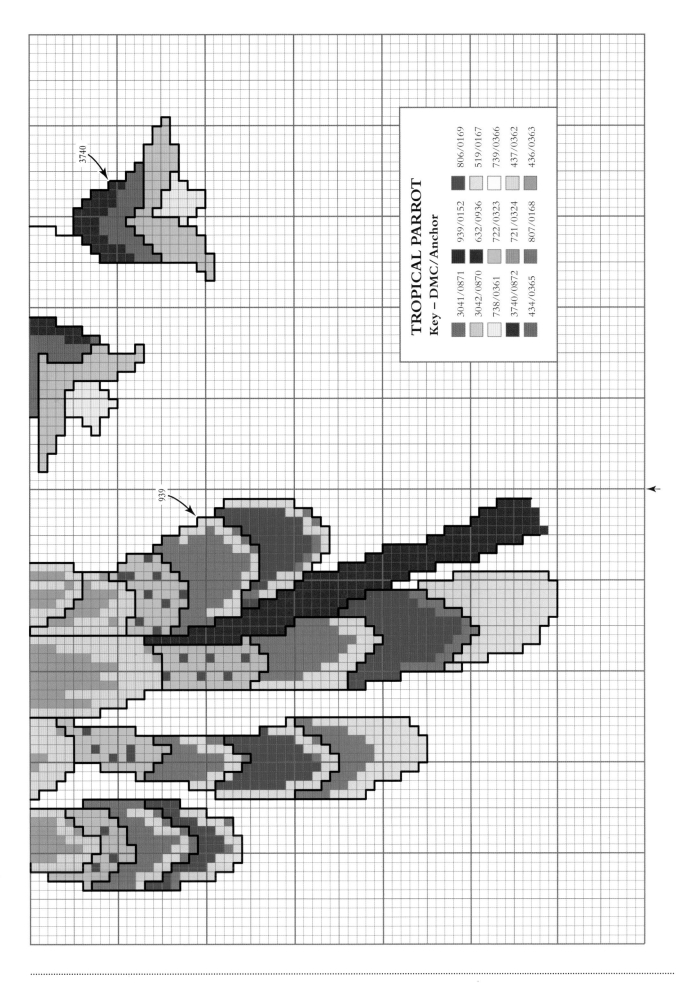

TROPICAL PARROT
Key – DMC/Anchor

3041/0871	939/0152	806/0169
3042/0870	632/0936	519/0167
738/0361	722/0323	739/0366
3740/0872	721/0324	437/0362
434/0365	807/0168	436/0363

3740

939

Tropical Parrot Picture

I have taken this design directly from the crewel panel illustrated in the background on page 123 by actually tracing the design onto tracing paper before squaring it off ready to stitch.

If you have not attempted designing yourself, this may be a good time to start. Look around at your home furnishings, including sofas, wall coverings, carpets and curtains, and you may see designs you could use as inspiration. When you select a motif to chart yourself, keep the tracing to simple clear lines – you can add detail when you stitch. To square off a line drawing tape the tracing to a glass window, cover with graph paper and redraw, following the original line but drawing in vertical or horizontal lines and keeping to the squares on the graph paper.

Skill Level 1

Stitch count: 87 x 123

Design size: 16 x 22 cm (6.25 x 8.75 inches)

Stitching notes: suitable for Aida and even-weave. Use two strands of stranded cotton (floss) for cross-stitch and one strand for back-stitch (optional).

YOU WILL NEED

28.5 x 35 cm (11.25 x 13.75 inches) oatmeal Aida, 14 blocks to 2.5 cm (1 inch)

Stranded cottons (floss) as listed on the chart

INSTRUCTIONS

Work a narrow hem around the edge of the Aida to prevent fraying. Fold into four, press lightly and, starting to the right of a vertical thread (see How to do a cross-stitch, page 22), mark the folds with a line of tacking (basting) stitches. Starting at the centre of the design, begin to stitch using two strands of stranded cotton for the cross-stitch working over one block.

Remember to keep the top stitch facing the same way and finish off the loose ends as you stitch by putting the needle to the back of the work and under stitches of the same or similar colour. Snip off the loose ends close to the stitching. Add the optional back-stitch, referring to the chart for suggested shade numbers.

When the stitching is complete, check for missed stitches and press lightly on the wrong side (see page 148). Make up as preferred (see pages 155–6).

Album Quilt

Album quilts were made all over the United States, but particularly in the South, during the nineteenth century and they are still being made today. These magnificent pieces of needlework were true samplers! They combined hand quilting, appliqué, patchwork and surface embroidery to great effect. It was common for a young woman to sit around with friends, making decorative squares and combining these stitched treasures in the final masterpiece. Album quilts are often referred to as 'friendship' quilts because of the relationships built up during the years it takes to complete them!

American Folk Art Cushions

The four cushions in this chapter are all based on quilt designs, have the same stitch count and are made to the same specifications, so I will include only one set of instructions.

The dimensions below do not include the fabric required to complete the cushions.

Cushion 1 – Fruit Basket
Cushion 2 – Cornucopia
Cushion 3 – Tulip Garland
Cushion 4 – Yellow House

Skill Level 1
Stitch count: 97 x 97
Design size: 18 cm (7 inches) square
Stitching notes: suitable for Aida and even weave. Use two strands of stranded cotton (floss) for the cross-stitch and one strand for the optional back-stitch.

You Will Need (Per Cushion)
1 25.5 cm (10 inch) square oatmeal Aida, 14 blocks to 2.5 cm (1 inch)
Stranded cottons (floss) as listed on the chart

Instructions
Work a narrow hem around the edge of the Aida to prevent fraying. Fold into four, press lightly and mark the folds with a line of tacking (basting) stitches. Starting at the centre of the design, begin to stitch using two strands of stranded cotton for the cross-stitch and working over one block.

Remember to keep the top stitch facing the same way and finish off the loose ends as you stitch by putting the needle to the back of the work and under stitches of the same or similar colour. Snip off the loose ends close to the stitching. Add the optional back-stitch referring to the chart for suggested shade numbers.

When the stitching is complete, check for missed stitches and press lightly on the wrong side (see page 148). Make up as preferred (see page 148).

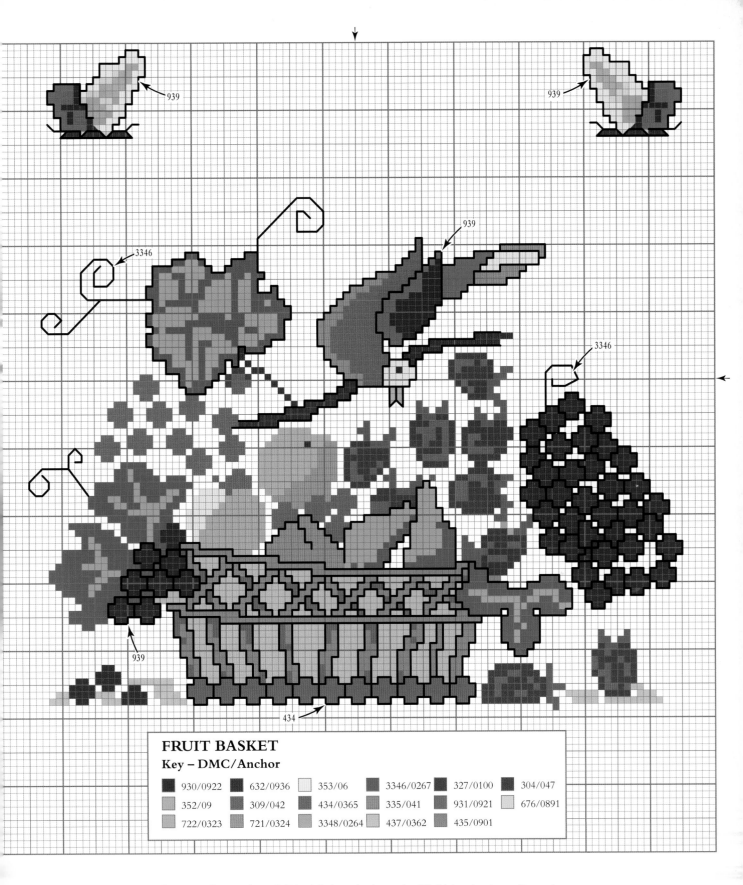

FRUIT BASKET
Key – DMC/Anchor

930/0922	632/0936	353/06	3346/0267	327/0100	304/047	
352/09	309/042	434/0365	335/041	931/0921	676/0891	
722/0323	721/0324	3348/0264	437/0362	435/0901		

The quartet of inset cushions (left) is stitched on a lovely tweedy Aida fabric and set in to a linen union.
These quilt designs would also look splendid as a set of four framed pictures.

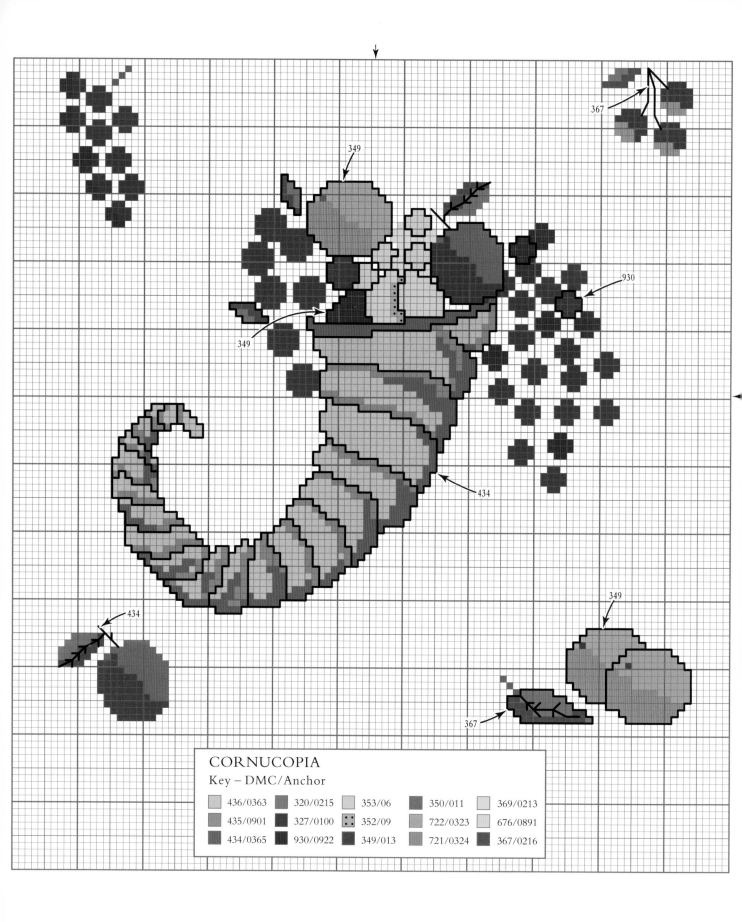

CORNUCOPIA
Key – DMC/Anchor

436/0363	320/0215	353/06
435/0901	327/0100	352/09
434/0365	930/0922	349/013

350/011	369/0213
722/0323	676/0891
721/0324	367/0216

349

367

930

434

434

349

367

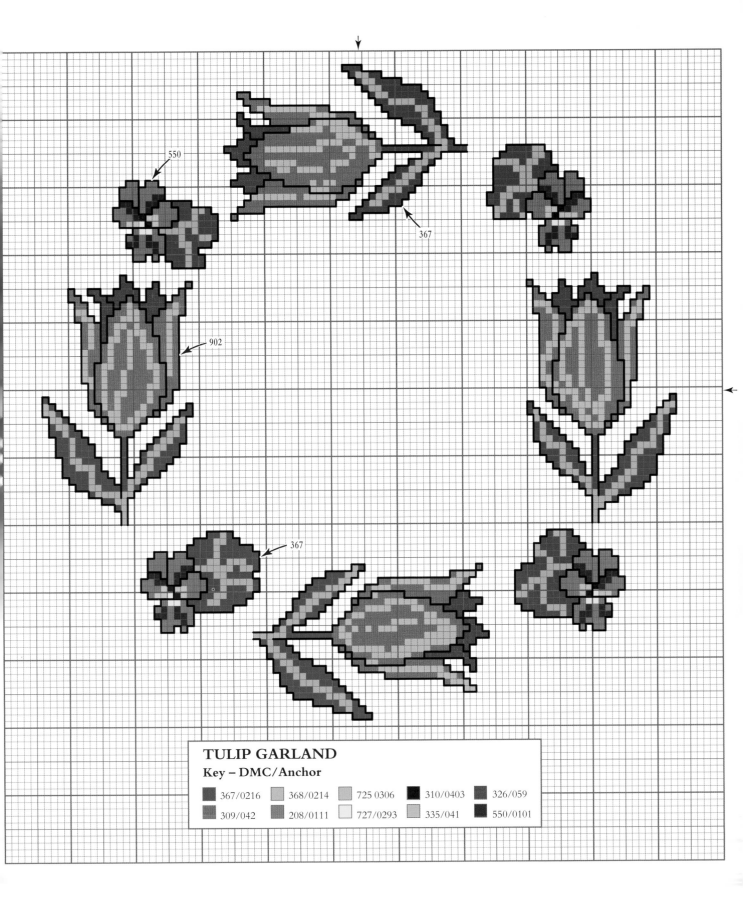

TULIP GARLAND

Key – DMC/Anchor

■	367/0216	■	368/0214	■	725 0306	■	310/0403	■	326/059
■	309/042	■	208/0111	■	727/0293	■	335/041	■	550/0101

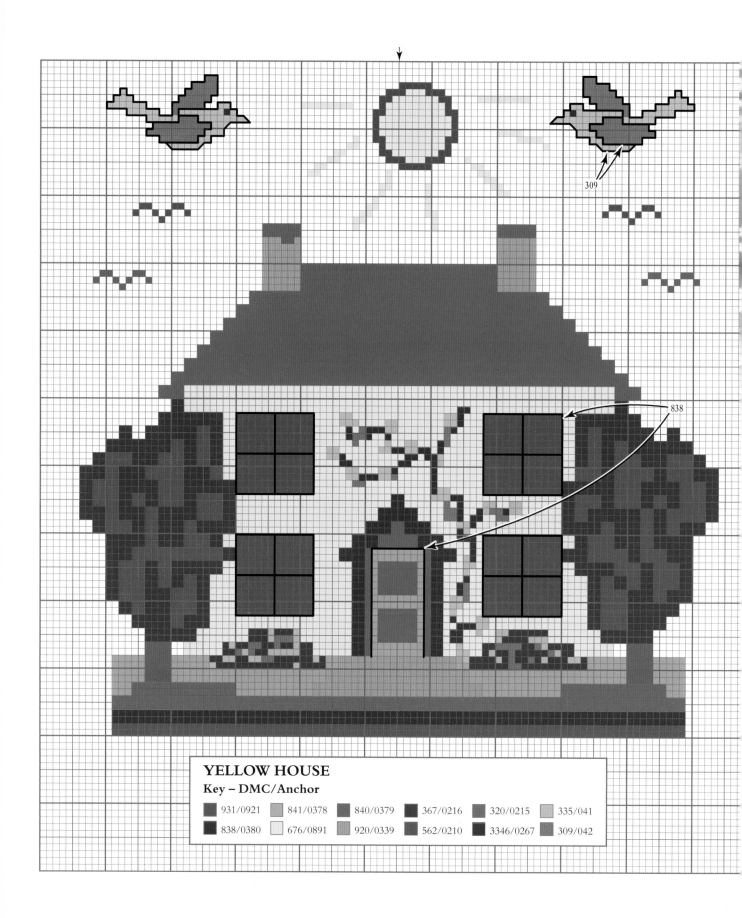

YELLOW HOUSE

Key – DMC/Anchor

931/0921	841/0378	840/0379	367/0216	320/0215	335/041
838/0380	676/0891	920/0339	562/0210	3346/0267	309/042

309

838

Band Sampler

As described earlier, the band sampler is one of the most fascinating areas of early embroidery. Although these long thin strips of linen were not intended to be decorative, they are now one of the most collectable types of needlework.
The chart on pages 138–9 is based on an early sampler, originally seen when the Bristol Sampler Collection was on loan to Cirencester Museum in Gloucestershire.
I have worked the band sampler illustrated on page 136 and adapted the design to make a few smaller items as shown in the pictures on pages 134 and 135.

Bible Cover

The Bible Cover is made in one section, so the fabric dimension indicated below allows for making up. The dimensions given below are for the bible pictured on page 134. Remember to adapt your fabric size to cover your chosen bible.

Skill Level 1
Stitch count: 68 x 83
Design size: 12.5 x 15 cm (5 x 6 inches)
Stitching notes: suitable for Aida or even weave fabric. Use two strands of stranded cotton (floss) for the cross-stitch over two threads on even weave or one block on Aida.

YOU WILL NEED
36 x 23 cm (14 x 9) inches beige Aida, 14 blocks to 2.5 cm (1 inch)
Stranded cottons (floss) as listed on the chart
Graph paper and soft pencil

INSTRUCTIONS
Work a narrow hem around the edge of the Aida to prevent fraying. Lay the fabric on a clean flat surface, long side towards you. Fold in half and then fold the top section in four and mark the folds with tacking threads. This will be the front of the Bible Cover. Set aside.

PLANNING A LAYOUT CHART
Before beginning this project, you will need to plan the position of each motif on graph paper (refer to Planning layout charts, page 21). It is not necessary to copy all the detail from the charts – use the outline only. The stitching can be worked from the colour charts when you have planned the correct motif positions.

When you are satisfied with your layout chart, start at the centre and begin to stitch using two strands of stranded cotton for the cross-stitch. Remember to keep the top stitch facing the same way and finish off the loose ends as you stitch by putting the needle to the back of the work and under stitches of the same or similar colour. Snip off the loose ends close to the stitching.

When the cross-stitch pattern is complete, carefully check for missed stitches, press lightly on the wrong side (see page 148), and make up as described in Making books on page 153.

Bible Bookmark

This small project is worked on fine Aida but would make an ideal design for linen or Aida band.

Skill Level 2

Stitch count: 29 x 66
Design size: 4 x 9 cm (1.5 x 3.5 inches)
Stitching notes: suitable for Aida or even weave. Use one strand of stranded cotton (floss) for the cross-stitch over one block on the Aida.

YOU WILL NEED
6.5 x 16.5 cm (2.5 x 6.5 inches) rustico, Aida 18 blocks to 2.5 cm (1 inch)
Stranded cottons (floss) as listed on the chart
Unbleached linen tassel
40 cm (16 inches) cotton bias binding for the trimming

INSTRUCTIONS
Work a narrow hem around the edge of the Aida to prevent fraying. Fold into four, press lightly and mark the folds with a line of tacking (basting) stitches.

Looking at the chart on pages 138–9, find the centre of the floral cross motif and begin to stitch at the centre, using one strand of stranded cotton for the cross-stitch. Add the small flower design centred below the cross.

When the cross-stitch pattern is complete, carefully check for missed stitches. Press lightly on the wrong side (see page 148) and make up with a simple bias binding edge as illustrated left (see also page 152). Add the tassel if desired.

These simple charming projects (left) are stitched on beige or rustico Aida in two different thread counts. I have added a purchased tassel to the Bookmark and a pretty ribbon to the Bible Cover.

Adam and Eve Sampler

Skill Level 1

Stitch count: 91 x 86
Design size: 16.5 x 16 cm (6.5 x 6.25 inches)
Stitching notes: suitable for Aida or even weave. Use two strands of stranded cotton (floss) for the cross-stitch and one for the back-stitch outline.

YOU WILL NEED
24 x 23 cm (9.5 x 9 inches) cream Aida, 14 blocks to 2.5 cm (1 inch)
Stranded cottons (floss) as listed on the chart

A simple cross-stitch project using a traditional sampler motif and counted alphabet.

INSTRUCTIONS

Follow the instructions for the Bible Cover working the design from the centre and keeping the top stitch facing the same direction. When the design is complete, check for missed stitches. Press lightly on the wrong side (see page 148) and mount and frame as desired (see pages 155–6).

Traditional Band Sampler

Skill Level 5

Stitch count: 83 x 243
Design size: 20 x 61 cm (8 x 24 inches)
Stitching notes: not suitable for Aida. Use three strands of stranded cotton (floss) for the cross-stitch and two for the back-stitch outline. Refer to the specific stitch instructions for each band as described opposite. All cross-stitch is worked over two threads of linen.

YOU WILL NEED

28 x 76 cm (11 x 30 inches) unbleached linen,
  20 threads to 2.5 cm (1 inch)
Stranded cottons (floss) as listed on the chart
1 skein DMC perle 5

INSTRUCTIONS

Work a narrow hem around the edge of the linen to prevent fraying. Fold into four, press lightly and, starting to the right of a vertical thread, mark the folds with a line of tacking (basting) stitches.

Starting at the centre of the design and to the left of a vertical thread (see How to do a cross-stitch,

page 21), begin to stitch using three strands of stranded cotton for the cross-stitch. Remember to keep the top stitch facing the same way and finish off the loose ends as you stitch.

Work each band as indicated on the chart on pages 138–9; refer to the Additional stitches section on page 23 if you are unsure.

BAND	STITCHES USED
1	Crowns in cross-stitch
2a	Floral cross in cross-stitch except for large pink roses. Work these in eyelet stitch (see page 85) over four threads using three strands of stranded cotton
3	Cross-stitch
4	Long stitch in four strands of stranded cotton
5	Herringbone stitch over four threads in three strands stranded cotton
6	Algerian eye over four threads using three strands of stranded cotton
7	Herringbone over four threads in three strands of stranded cotton
8	Adam and Eve panel in cross-stitch
9	Alphabet in cross-stitch
10	Cross-stitch in one strand of perle 5
11	Hemstitch, drawn threads and somersault stitch in perle 5
12	Hemstitch in one strand of perle 5
13	Algerian eye in one strand of perle 5 over four threads
14	Cross-stitch

When the project is complete, press lightly on the wrong side (see page 148) and frame as preferred (see pages 155–6).

This elegant band sampler includes some beautiful old-fashioned stitches as well as cross-stitch. An ideal project to try experimenting with your needle.

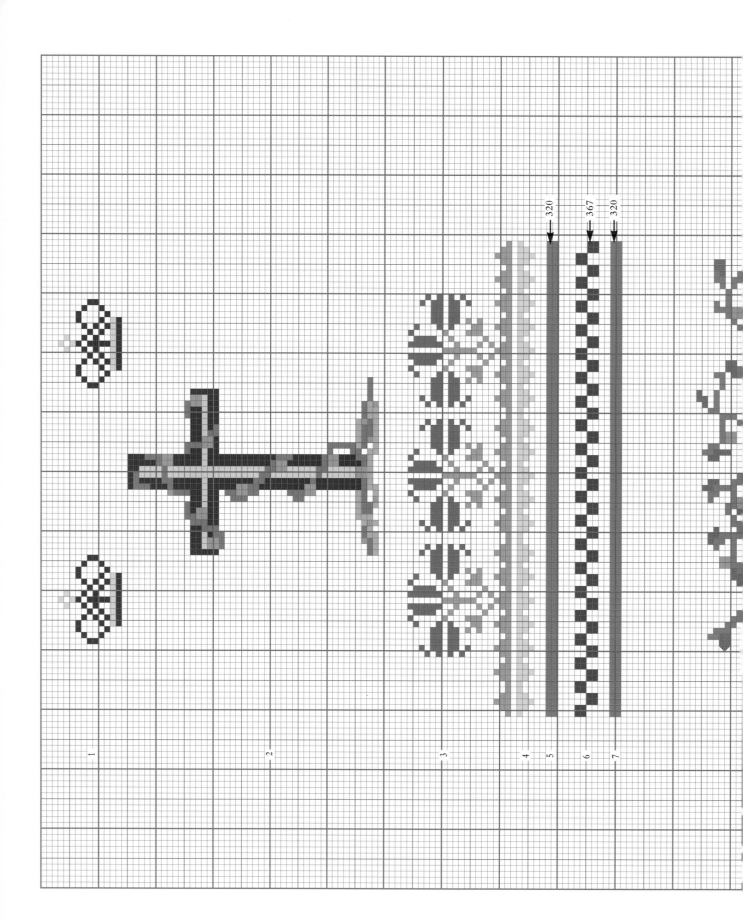

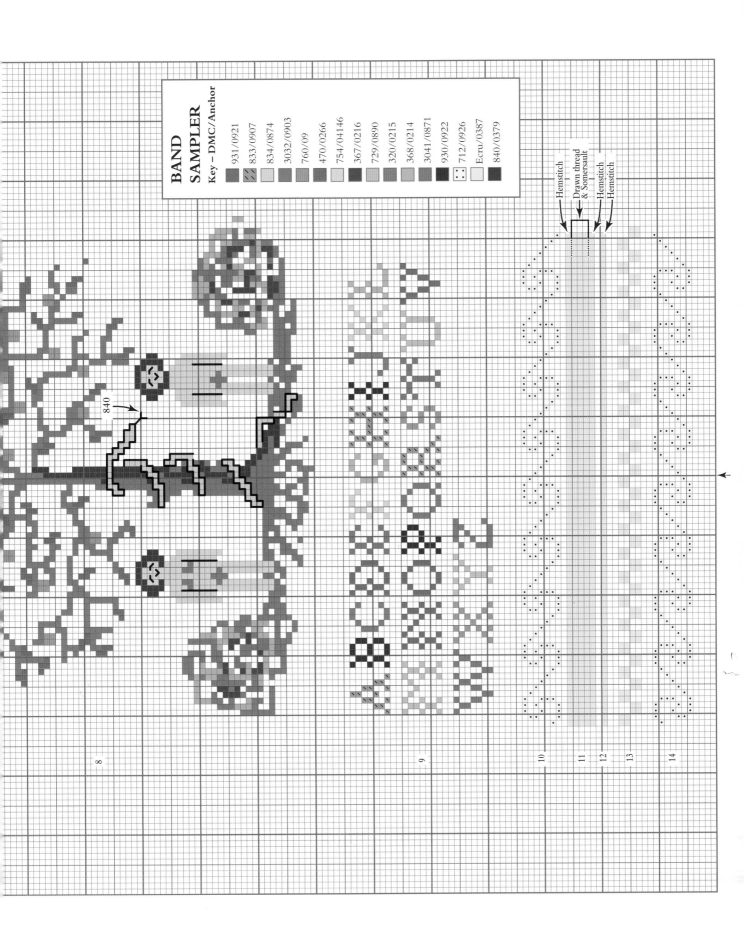

BAND SAMPLER

Key – DMC/Anchor

931/0921
833/0907
834/0874
3032/0903
760/09
470/0266
754/04146
367/0216
729/0890
320/0215
368/0214
3041/0871
930/0922
712/0926
Ecru/0387
840/0379

840

Hemstitch
Drawn thread & Somersault
Hemstitch
Hemstitch

8

9

10

11

12

13

14

Spot Motif Sampler

As discussed on page 36 spot motif samplers are ideal inspiration for modern stitchers. This chapter is based on designs stitched during the seventeenth century in Britain and are part of the collection of textiles at the Embroiderers' Guild at Hampton Court Palace.
As mentioned before random patterns or motifs were commonly stitched during this period and used as pieces of appliqué. These designs are ideal for decorating a card, trinket pot or even a clock (see illustration on page 142).

Random Spot Sampler

There are a few three-quarter stitches in this design, so refer to Additional stitches on page 26 before you start. Add the back-stitch outline *after* the cross-stitch is complete as this will enable you to perfect the appearance of the stitching.

Skill Level 3
Stitch count: 126 x 105
Design size: 23 x 19 cm (9.5 x 7.5 inches)
Stitching notes: not suitable for Aida. Use an even-weave fabric. Use two strands of stranded cotton (floss) for the cross-stitch over two threads on even-weave.

You Will Need
35.5 x 32 cm (14 x 12.5 inches) Jobelan sage,
  28 threads to 2.5 cm (1 inch)
Stranded cottons (floss) as listed on the chart

Instructions
Work a narrow hem around the edge of the linen to prevent fraying. Fold into four, press lightly and mark the folds with a line of tacking (basting)

stitches. Following the chart on pages 144–5, start in the centre and begin to the left of a vertical thread working the cross-stitch over two threads of the linen in all cases.

Work the Algerian eye in two strands of stranded cotton over four threads of the fabric (see Additional stitches, page 24), remembering to keep any loose threads away from the hole in the centre of each stitch. The stitch is a 'pulled' stitch and is one of the few occasions where you should make the hole in the fabric larger as you stitch!

Remember to keep the top stitch facing the same way and finish off the loose ends as you stitch by putting the needle to the back of the work and under stitches of the same or similar colour. Snip off the loose ends close to the stitching.

When the cross-stitch pattern is complete, carefully check for missed stitches and press lightly on the wrong side (see page 148). Mount and frame as preferred (see pages 155–6).

This elegant picture made up of random motifs includes cross-stitch and Algerian eye stitches. The pretty, stylized example of the peacock would make a lovely motif for a card or trinket pot.

Mantel Clock

This simple modern-looking design is worked to fit a bought wooden clock as illustrated. Please check the dimensions of your clock before beginning to stitch (see Calculating design size, page 20). The dimensions and fabric requirements are given for the example in the colour picture.

Skill Level 2
Stitch count: 42 x 66
Design size: 7.5 x 12 cm (3 x 4.75 inches)
Stitching notes: suitable for Aida or an even-weave fabric. Use two strands of stranded cotton (floss) for the cross-stitch over two threads on even weave.

YOU WILL NEED
12.5 x 17 cm (5 x 6.75 inches) Jobelan beige,
  28 threads to 2.5 cm (1 inch)
Stranded cottons (floss) as listed on the chart
Graph paper
Soft pencil

INSTRUCTIONS
Work a narrow hem around the edge of the fabric to prevent fraying. Fold into four, press lightly and, starting to the right of a vertical thread (see Where to start, page 23), mark the folds with a line of tacking (basting) stitches. Set aside.

PLANNING A LAYOUT CHART
Before beginning this project, you will need to plan the position of each motif on graph paper (refer to Planning layout charts, page 21). It is not necessary to copy all the detail from the charts – use the outline only. The stitching can be worked from the colour charts when you have planned the correct motif positions. I have selected the group of heart shapes (see middle, top of the photograph of the Spot Motif Sampler on page 141). For the clock project I have 'exploded' the motif and positioned the spindle for the hands in the centre.

Draw the clock stitch count as a box on your graph paper using 42 by 66 squares. Mark the positions of the spindle for the clock hands on the graph paper and add the numbers next. Select the numbers required from the chart on pages 144–5, positioning the '12' and '6' at the top and bottom and the '9' and '3' either side of the spindle.

Add the outlines of the selected motifs and check the overall effect. When you are satisfied, start at the centre and begin to cross-stitch following the coloured chart and using two strands of stranded cotton. Add the numbers in back-stitch, using one strand of stranded cotton. Add the Algerian eye stitches as illustrated, referring to page 24 for additional instructions if you have not attempted these before.

Remember to keep the top stitch facing the same way and finish off the loose ends as you stitch by putting the needle to the back of the work and under stitches of the same or similar colour. Snip off the loose ends close to the stitching.

When the design is complete, check for missed stitches and make up as instructed by the manufacturer's instructions.

This handsome, purchased mantel clock includes motifs from the Random Spot Sampler and is worked on beige Jobelan. I have used the four heart shapes around the clock spindle and the Algerian eye patterns to form corner motifs.

3346

939

Algerian eye

939

434

353

Algerian eye

3346

309

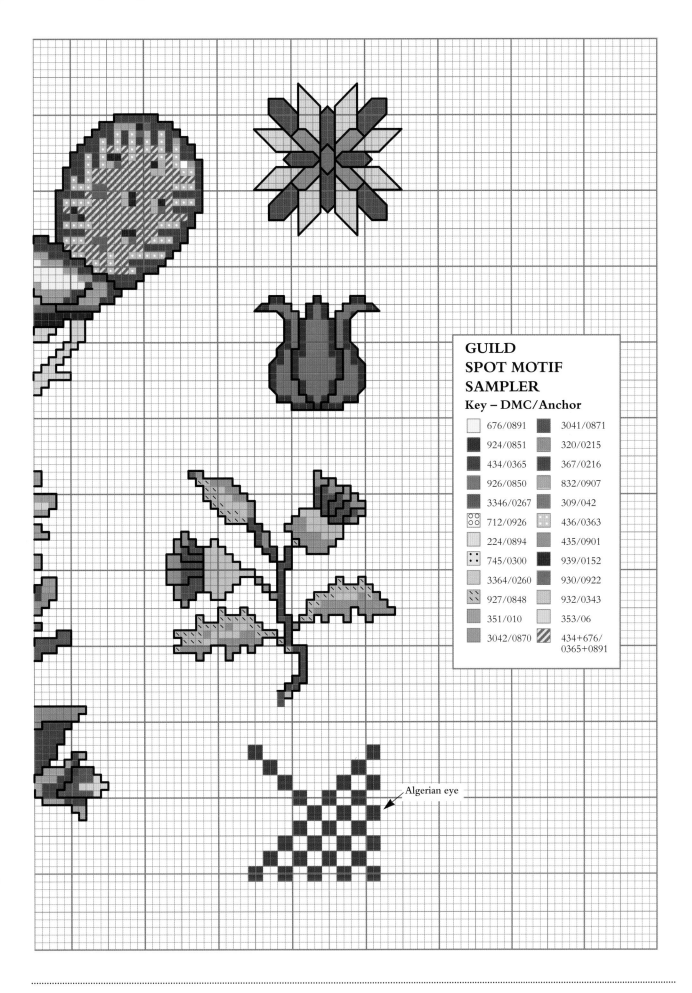

GUILD
SPOT MOTIF
SAMPLER
Key – DMC/Anchor

	676/0891		3041/0871
	924/0851		320/0215
	434/0365		367/0216
	926/0850		832/0907
	3346/0267		309/042
	712/0926		436/0363
	224/0894		435/0901
	745/0300		939/0152
	3364/0260		930/0922
	927/0848		932/0343
	351/010		353/06
	3042/0870		434+676/ 0365+0891

Algerian eye

Perfecting
Treasures

Finishing Techniques

Washing and Pressing Cross-stitch

When a piece of cross-stitch is complete, it may be necessary to wash the item before finishing. Washing can give a piece of stitching new life, but can also ruin your work if care is not taken. Drinks, ice-cream and cats can cause havoc so always keep your stitching covered and away from all of them.

If it does become necessary to wash a piece of stitching, DMC or Anchor threads are usually colourfast, though some reds can bleed, so always check for colourfastness before immersing the project completely. To do this, dampen a white tissue and press the red stitches at the back of the work. Lift the tissue and look for any traces of red colour. If any colour is visible on the tissue, avoid washing this project.

If the item is colourfast, wash it using bleach-free soap and hand-hot water, squeezing gently but never rubbing. Rinse in plenty of warm water and dry naturally. Do not use a tumble dryer.

To iron cross-stitch, heat the iron to a hot setting and use the steam button if your iron has one. Cover the ironing board with a thick layer of towelling. Place the stitching on the towelling, right side down with the back of the work facing you. Press the fabric quite firmly and you will see how much this improves the appearance of your stitching. Leave the embroidery to cool and dry completely before framing or making up.

Ageing Linen

It is easy to add 'age' to a piece of linen or lace by dipping it in warm black tea. It is possible to age a completed piece of needlework by dipping the whole thing in black tea, although you must check if the colours are fast before you attempt this. After dipping the needlework, allow to dry naturally and press as described above.

Making Up

Many of the designs in this book can be made up into items for the home and not only as framed pictures but as cushions, purses and pincushions.

Making Inset Cushions

This section deals with making inset cushions, both piped and frilled, scissor- and key-keepers.

Pipe-edged Cushion
(See American Folk Art Cushions, page 127.)

YOU WILL NEED
50 cm (20 inches) furnishing fabric
Piping cord, enough to go round outside edge of cushion fabric (allow extra for turning)
Cushion pad about 5 cm (2 inches) larger than the finished cushion

Frilled Cushion
(See Coffee and Cream Lace Brooch Pillow, page 41.)

YOU WILL NEED
70 cm (28 inches) fabric, fine enough to gather easily
Cushion pad about 5 cm (2 inches) larger than the finished cushion

INSTRUCTIONS
The seam allowance throughout is 1.25 cm (0.5 inches). Measure the embroidery and decide on the size you would like the finished cushion to be. Subtract the embroidery measurement from the finished measurement, divide this by two and add on two seam allowances. This gives you the width for the border pieces.

Using the cutting plans (shown below), cut all the pieces. Trim the fabric to within 2.5 cm (1 inch) of the embroidery and mark it with a pin. Pin the border panels to the embroidery, matching the centre points and leaving the ends loose. Machine-stitch these seams using a piping foot, taking care that the machine stitches meet at each corner.

If you now fold the embroidery in half, diagonally and wrong sides together, you will find it easy to mitre the corners by stitching a line from the corner of the embroidery to the corner of the border panels (see below). Trim the excess cloth on this seam and clip the corners. Repeat, folding on the other diagonal, to mitre the other two corners.

To inset small items like pincushions or scissorkeepers, use the method as above allowing smaller margins.

Cutting plan – piped version

Cutting plan – frilled version

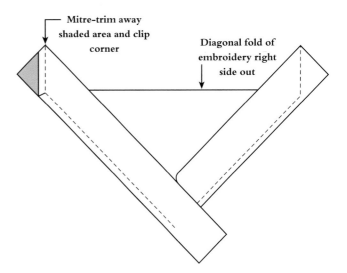

Mitre the border

PIPED VERSION
Use a piping foot to make the piping and attach piping to the outer edge of the front. Make a join at the bottom. Lay the back piece over the front, right sides together, and stitch working tightly against the piping and leaving an opening at the bottom edge to insert the cushion pad. Turn the right sides out, insert the pad and slip-stitch the opening to finish off the cushion.

FRILLED VERSION

Seam the frill pieces together to make a continuous loop and fold this in half, right sides out. Run gathers along the raw edges and pull up to fit the outer edge of the cushion. Pin the frill to the edge of the front, spreading the gathers evenly, with the folded edges facing the centre of the cushion. Stitch this seam. Pin the back to the front with the right sides together. Stitch, leaving an opening to insert the cushion pad. Turn right sides out, insert the pad and slip-stitch the opening.

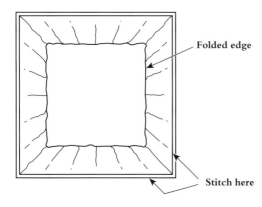

Frilled version

Folded edge

Stitch here

Appliquéd Cushion

(See the Checked Alphabet Cushion on page 78.)

The cushion is made using the same method as the pipe-edged version described above, but the needlework is attached to the front panel by machine and decorated with the antique lace.

The Four Seasons Floor Cushion

This bright and cheerful patchwork cushion is made up of the four Amish panels, joined together with 7.5 cm (3 inches) strips of linen union and then made up as the piped version described above.

Scissor- and Key-keepers

YOU WILL NEED

A small quantity of the yarn used for the design to make twisted cord
A small quantity of polyester stuffing

INSTRUCTIONS

Make a 30-cm (12-inch) length of twisted cord (see page 153). Trim the stitching to within 1 cm (0.375 inches) of the embroidery and fold the edges in. Folding in the raw edges as you stitch, work a row of long-legged cross-stitch by taking one thread from each side of the join. This way the embroidery will form a seam as well as decorating the edge. Fill the keeper with polyester stuffing and tuck in the two ends of the cord to make a loop before finishing the seam completely. Add any bows, ribbons or trimmings as desired.

Beaded Initial Jewel Case

YOU WILL NEED

1 piece 19 x 25.5 cm (7.5 x 10 inches) red fabric
1 piece 19 x 43 cm (7.5 x 17 inches) red fabric (or matching lining)
1 metre (39.5 inches) satin bias binding
Polyester wadding

INSTRUCTIONS

Using sharp scissors, round the corners of the stitched section slightly (see photograph on page 80). Set aside. Take the smaller piece of red fabric and place on a clean flat surface. This will form the back of the case. With right sides together, pin the stitching to the narrow edge of the back section and machine-stitch. Press seam open. Lay the embroidery on a clean flat surface and set aside.

Cut a piece of polyester wadding using the stitched piece as a pattern. Lay the stitched piece face down on a clean flat surface with the stitching

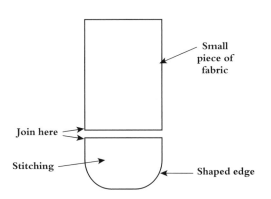

Joining the back section

at the top. Cover with a piece of wadding and then the remaining piece of red fabric. Pin and tack through all layers. Trim away any excess.

Use the bias binding according to the method described on page 152 and bind the short edge nearest to you. Make a fold a third of the way along and fold up the bound edge to make a pocket. Match raw edges and pin into position. To join the pocket sides bind the edges together with the bias binding starting at the fold, continuing around the curved section and finishing at the other side of the fold.

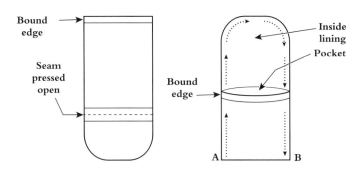

Add bias binding following arrows from A to B

Crazy Panel Spectacle Case

YOU WILL NEED
Black velvet
Bias binding

INSTRUCTIONS
Make up the front section as for the small inset cushion. Follow the instructions set out in the Beaded Initial Jewel Case for the bias binding and use it as the hanging cord.

Violet-scented Sachet

YOU WILL NEED
Piece of matching fabric the same size as the stitching for the back of the sachet
Piece of narrow cream lace to trim the outside edges
Ribbon or fabric for a bow
Scented pot pourri or polyester wadding

INSTRUCTIONS
To complete the sachet, place the finished stitching and the back section with right sides together and pin into position. Join the side seams, matching raw edges together. Turn right side out, press lightly and trim the raw edge with lace. Stuff with pot pourri or wadding and slip-stitch to close. Add ribbon bow.

Appliquéd Letter Satchel

YOU WILL NEED
33 x 21.5 cm (13 x 8.5 inches) piece of blue suede
3 strips of dark blue suede for edge panels
46 x 21.5 cm (18 x 8.5 inches) piece of blue lining fabric

INSTRUCTIONS
Place the stitched piece on a clean flat surface right side up with the bottom edge nearest you. Taking a strip of suede, pin to the bottom edge with right

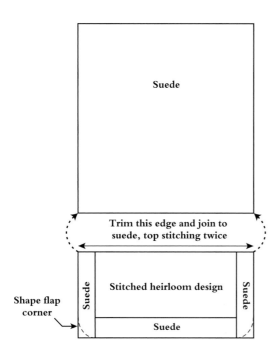

Stitching plan for Letter Satchel

sides together and machine. Open out the seam and repeat for the two side sections (see diagram). Trim along the top of the linen and suede. With sharp scissors, carefully shape the stitched flap to round the corners slightly.

Join the stitched section and the remaining suede along the narrow edge, top-stitching twice. Place

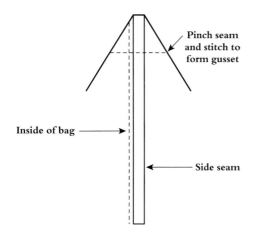

Pinch side seam and stitch to form gusset

this completed section on a clean flat surface, right side up and cover with lining fabric. Pin into position and machine around the edge, leaving a small section to allow for turning.

Turn the project the right way out and carefully press the seams. Make a fold a third of the way and fold up the narrow raw edge (right sides together) to make a pocket. Match the edges and pin into position. Join the pocket sides, start at the fold and machine through all the layers. To form a gusset, pinch the bottom corner of the side seam and stitch as illustrated. Repeat for the other side.

Fruit Tree Needlecase

YOU WILL NEED
Matching threads to make a twisted cord
17 x 23 cm (6.75 x 9 inches) felt or flannel for pages

INSTRUCTIONS
Place the completed stitching on a clean flat surface, right side up. Cover with lining fabric, right sides together, and pin into position. Machine round all four sides but leave a small opening for turning. Turn right side out, slip-stitch opening and press. Cut two felt pages, fold in half and slip inside the book. Make a twisted cord and tie around the spine, thus attaching the pages.

Bias Binding

Some of the projects in this book are completed using bias binding, which can be purchased or home-made. To attach bias binding simply and quickly, by hand or machine, proceed as follows. Cut the binding to the correct length. Pin and stitch the binding to the wrong side of the project first, matching the raw edges. Fold the binding to the right side and top-stitch into position. Press lightly.

Making Twisted Cords

Follow this method for the cords you see on the finished projects in the book, using stranded cotton (floss) for all the projects except for the Braided Sampler Cushion for which an Appleton key is included.

Choose a colour or group of colours in stranded cottons to match the stitching. Cut a minimum of four lengths, at least four times the finished length required. Fold in half. Ask a friend to hold the two ends, while you slip a pencil through the loop at the other end. Twist the pencil and continue twisting until kinks appear. Walk slowly towards your partner and the cord will twist automatically. Smooth out the kinks from the looped end and tie another knot at the other end to secure.

Twist

Twist until very tight then fold back in half

Making Books

I use the scoring method to make books, which allows the book to be made in one piece. You will need a piece of stiff card large enough to make the front, back and spine of the book.

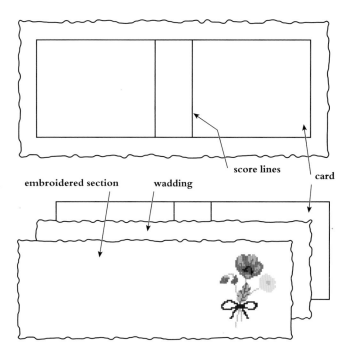

score lines

card

embroidered section   **wadding**

Making books by the scoring method

Lay the card on a clean flat surface and, using a sharp craft knife, score as illustrated above. Fold the card thus forming the spine. Lay the card on a clean flat surface and cover with a piece of wadding slightly larger than the card. Sandwich this to the card with the embroidery, checking the position of the stitching.

Using the pinning method described in Stretching and mounting on page 155, pin into position. Trim the excess material away leaving 2.5 cm (1 inch) around the edge and secure this with strips of double-sided tape. Pressing gently on the scored areas as you do it, fold the front and back up to check that the fabric is secure and then set aside while the lining is prepared.

Cut a piece of co-ordinating material for the lining at least 2.5 cm (1 inch) larger than the completed book, fold the raw edges inside and slip-stitch into position.

Covered Mounts

This section is used for the photograph frames and the Stuart Mirror on page 100 to co-ordinate with the design. If you intend to use an oval or circular shaped mount, you will certainly need to buy it as to cut these yourself is almost impossible. Square or rectangular mounts can be cut using a craft knife as the rough edges will be covered by the material.

Press the embroidery on the wrong side and stretch and mount as described below. Cut the mount card the same size as the mounted embroidery and cut an opening of the size you require. If the mount has been purchased, check the opening is large enough for the embroidery and set aside.

Using the mount as a template cut a piece of fabric or the cross-stitch project at least 2.5 cm (1 inch) wider all the way around (see diagram). Place the material right side down on a clean flat surface and, using a soft pencil, draw around the inside of the opening. Remove the mount and use a sharp pair of pointed scissors to cut out an opening of about 1.25 cm (0.5 inch) from the pencil line. Clip the edge at intervals.

On the wrong side of the mount apply a thin layer of adhesive to the edge of the opening (see diagram) and add the material, checking the design is in the right position. Stick down and leave to dry.

Complete the procedure by pinning and securing the excess material as described in Stretching and mounting opposite.

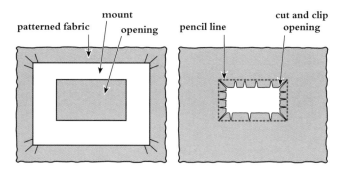

Covered mounts – stages 1 and 2

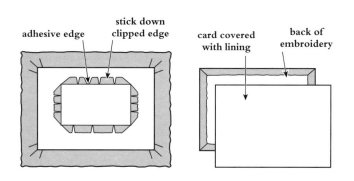

Covered mounts – stages 3 and 4

Footstools and Pincushions

The basic principles for making any padded projects are very similar. Pincushions and footstools are made in the same way but to different scales. Press the cross-stitch on the wrong side and set aside. Remove the screw from underneath the wooden base and remove the pad.

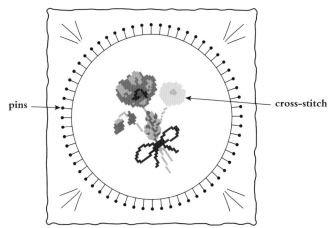

Placing pins around the edge of the footstool or pincushion base

Lay the stitched piece on top of the pad, check the position and carefully pin round the edge as illustrated, pulling firmly and gradually to remove any creases or folds. Trim away any excess fabric and lace the remainder under the base. When complete, place back in the wooden surround and replace the screw.

Stretching and Mounting

When mounting small cards or novelty projects, the whole procedure can be completed using double-sided sticky tape, but it is worth taking more time and effort on larger projects.

You will need one of the following: an acid-free mounting board, a lightweight foam board or possibly a piece of board covered with a natural fabric like cotton, which can be fixed with a rubber-based adhesive and left to dry.

There are three methods of attaching the needlework to the board before framing:
1 Pin the work to the edge of the board and stick in place with double-sided tape.
2 Pin to a covered board and stitch into position.

3 Pin to the board and lace across the back with strong linen thread.

When you pin the material to the board, it must be centred and stretched evenly because any wobbles will show when the design is framed. Measure the board across the bottom edge and mark the centre with a pin. Match this to the centre of the bottom edge of the embroidery and, working outwards from the centre, pin through the fabric following a line of threads until all four sides are complete. Either stitch through the needlework to the covered board, lace the excess material across the back or fix with double-sided tape.

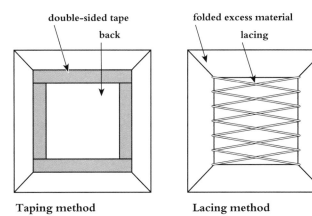

Taping method   **Lacing method**

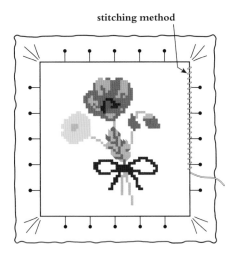

Stitching method

Framing

You will see from the wonderful colour photographs earlier in the book how the frame can greatly affect the end appearance of the design. Professional framing can be very expensive, particularly if you want something a little different. Most of the framing and finishing techniques suggested in this book can be tackled by the amateur at home – this will save you a lot of money.

When choosing a frame for a particular project, select the largest moulding you can afford and do not worry if the colour is not suitable. Buy the-frame, glass, etc. in kit form (most framers do not mind) and then decorate the frame yourself.

Painting Frames and Mounts

I use readily available products such as car spray paint! (You can buy this from car repair or body shop suppliers.) There are hundreds of colours in the range but if you have no luck, try bicycle paint which has an even greater selection! For subtle matt shades explore the endless possibilities with emulsion paints from DIY shops, often available in tiny tester sizes which are ideal for trial and error.

Before you begin to paint a piece of moulding, take care to cover all nearby surfaces with paper or dust cloths (spray paint goes everywhere!). If the moulding is completely untreated, rub down gently with fine sand paper, clean with white spirit on a soft cloth and allow to dry completely.

If using spray paint, try the spray on a sheet of waste paper first to perfect the technique. It is better to add a number of light coats rather than one thick layer. Experiment until you find a colour or combination of colours which suit the stitching, and allow to dry completely.

When the paint is dry, you may wish to add a 'distressed' look to the frame, which can be achieved by rubbing the moulding with sand paper to reveal bare wood or adding polishes to the grooves in the frame. Great effects can be achieved by using contrasting-coloured polishes, liming wax, acrylic paints or matt varnish. When you are satisfied with the effect, it is time to assemble the complete project.

Assembling Frames

Ensure that the stitching is selected and mounted properly (see page 155) and set aside. Place the frame face down on a covered surface and after carefully cleaning both sides of the glass with mirror or glass cleaner, place the glass in the frame rebate and insert the gold slip. A slip is an additional thin piece of moulding, cut to fit the frame, which is usually inserted to add depth and dimension to a frame. It also prevents damage to your stitching.

Adding a Mount (Mat)

As you will see from the colour picture of the Crazy Patchwork Sampler on page 109, adding a decorated mount (mat) can add dimension to very simple projects and you could even try spray-painting the mount to co-ordinate with the colour of the frame. For the Wild Rose Photograph Frame I have added a stitched mount to decorate the photograph, but this technique may be used to add excitement to any piece of stitching.

Bibliography and Further Reading

Samplers: Five Centuries of a Gentle Craft
Anne Sebba (Wiedenfeld & Nicolson, 1979)
Three Hundred Years of Embroidery 1600–1900
Pauline Johnstone (Wakefield Press, 1986)
Treasures of the Embroiderers' Guild
Edited by Elizabeth Benn (David & Charles, 1991)
Raised Embroidery
Barbara and Roy Hurst (Merehurst Ltd, 1993)
Antique Needlework
Lanto Synge (Blandford, 1982)
Samplers and Samplemakers
Mary Jaene Edmonds (Letts, 1991)
The following private publications are available from good needlework shops:
A Notebook of Sampler Stitches by Eileen Bennet
Hardanger: Basics and Beyond by Janice Love
Seventeenth-century Band Sampler by Meg Shinall (Gloria & Pat)

Suppliers

Linens and Afghans

Fabric Flair Ltd, The Old Brewery, The Close, Warminster, Wiltshire, England BA12 9AL.
Tel: 0800 716851
Wichelt Imports, Rural Route 1, Stoddard, WI 54658, USA. Tel: +608 788 4600
Stadia Handcrafts, P.O. Box 495, 85 Elizabeth Street, Paddington, NSW 2021, Australia.
Tel: +612 328 7973

Liberty Fabrics

Liberty plc, 210–20 Regent Street, London W1R 6AH UK. Tel: 0171 734 1234
Liberty of London Inc., 108 West 39th Street, New York, NY 10018, USA. Tel: +212 459 0080
Norman Vivian Pty Ltd, 18 Belmore Street, Surry Hills, NSW 2010, Australia. Tel: +612 212 1633

Threads and Fabrics

DMC Creative World Ltd, Pullman Road, Wigston, Leicestershire LE18 2DY UK.
Tel: 01162 811040
DMC Corporation, Port Kearny, Building 10, South Kearny, New Jersey 07032, USA.
Tel: +201 589 0606
DMC Needlecraft Pty Ltd, P.O. Box 317, Earlwood, NSW, Australia. Tel: +612 559 3088

Collections for inspiration

If you would like further information about the sources of inspiration for this book, please contact the museums and houses listed below.

The Museum of American Folk Art, New York, USA Tel:+212 977 7298
The Burrell Collection, Glasgow, Scotland Tel: 0141 649 7151
City Museum of Rotterdam, Holland Tel:+311 047 61 533
The Victoria & Albert Museum, London, England Tel: 0171 938 8500
Kelmscott Manor, Kelmscott, Oxfordshire, England Tel: 01367 252486
Parham House, Storrington, Sussex, England Tel: 01903 742021
Germanisches Nationalmuseum, Nuremberg, Germany Tel:+49 911 133 10
Montacute House, Somerset, England Tel: 01935 826294
County Museum of Art, Los Angeles, USA Tel:+213 857 6000
Norsk Folkmuseum, Oslo, Norway Tel:+47 22 43 70 20
Sudeley Castle, Gloucestershire, England Tel: 01242 602308
The Art Institute, Chicago, USA Tel:+312 4433600
Hatfield House, Hertfordshire, England Tel: 01707 262823
Philadelphia Museum of Art, Philadelphia, USA Tel:+215 763 8100
Bristol City Museum, Avon, England Tel: 01179 223571
The Embroiderers' Guild, Hampton Court, England Tel: 0181 943 1229
The Cameron Trading Post, Arizona, USA Tel:+520 679 2231

Index